WITHDRAWN

D1029227

THE WORLD OF MARCEL PROUST

ANDRÉ MAUROIS

THE WORLD OF MARCEL PROUST

Translated from the French by Moura Budberg
with the assistance of Barbara Creed
special photographs and research by André Ostier

HARPER & ROW, PUBLISHERS
New York / Evanston / San Francisco / London

For information address Harper & Row, Publishers, Inc.,
10 East 53rd Street, New York, N.Y. 10022.

FIRST U.S. EDITION 1974
ISBN 0-06-012864-X
LIBRARY OF CONGRESS CATALOG CARD NUMBER 74-5793

Designed by David Chaston
Conceived and edited by Felix Brenner

Printed in Great Britain by
W S Cowell Limited
Ipswich

Filmset by BAS Printers Limited,
Wallop, Hampshire, England

In the beginning was Illiers.

A small town near Chartres on the

Each year on the Thursday before Easter, the Proust family left Paris for Illiers, a little town epitomised by the church of Saint Jacques. Having quickly left the train from Chartres, rugs and parcels in hand they crossed the viaduct and hurried to 'Tante Léonie's' house down the street to the left.

border between La Beauce and Perche, the private, temporal seat of Paradise on Earth. For centuries, there had been Prousts living there, old, respected stock with roots deep in the countryside. A child spending his holidays in Illiers would find there the ancient French town, the old church, secure beneath its bell-tower, the rich, provincial accent, the mysterious code of manners and all the qualities of the 'Français de Saint-André-des-Champs' whose faces, sculpted in stone in mediaeval times over porches and on pillars,

On market day, Friday, and on Sunday the square thronged with people. The rest of the time, it was empty save for strollers and those on errands; the patient days punctuated by the quarter hours rung from the belfry.

can still be seen, unchanged, in shop doorways, in the markets and in the fields.

In the course of time, the Prousts knew diverse fortunes. One of them, in 1633, became manorial dues collector to the Marquis d'Illiers in return for a yearly payment of ten thousand five hundred pounds minted at Tours and the obligation of 'supplying a candle every year to the church of Notre Dame de Chartres on the feasts of Notre Dame de la Chandeleur.' Of his descendants, some were

tradespeople and others farmers but the family always retained its link with the church and then, at the beginning of the 19th century, a Proust, grandfather of 'our' Proust, was candle and taper maker in Illiers. In the old rue de Cheval-Blanc, you can still see the door of the house where Marcel's grandfather François was born, a rough and rustic dwelling, with sandstone steps under an arch 'that seems to be the work of a sculptor of gothic images even to the stone from which he might have made his cribs and calvaries.' François Proust moved to 11, place Marché in 1827 and there two children

Grandfather Proust's shop was number 11 in the market place, just opposite the church, where he made and sold candles, wax, honey, chocolate and vanilla and dealt in spices, cotton, pottery, glass bottles and crystal, hardware, spirits and liqueurs. Oncle Amiot's drapers shop was at 14, on the right, with the grille-work balcony.

were born, a son, Adrien, and earlier, a daughter Elisabeth who married Jules Amiot, the most respected tradesman in Illiers. Monsieur Amiot owned a shop of novelties in the square 'which people used to visit before Mass and were welcomed by a delicious smell of unbleached linen.' In years to come, after lengthy incantations, Tante Amiot was to be transformed into Tante Léonie for her nephew and for the whole world. Her home, a very simple one, in the rue du Saint-Esprit, had two entrances, as in the novel: the front door, through which Françoise used to go to Camus' grocery and which faced the house of Madame Goupil, that Madame Goupil who 'got soaked to the skin' going to Vespers in her silk dress; and the back door on to the tiny garden where, in the evenings the Prousts and the Amiots sitting in front of the house under the great chestnut tree, could hear the low, metallic screech of the door that 'intimate friends used without ringing', or the hesitant, double tinkle of the little golden oval bell that was for strangers.

Adrien Proust, father of 'our' Proust, was the first of his blood to leave La Beauce. His father, the candlemaker, had intended him for the priesthood. He won a scholarship to the Collège de Chartres but soon abandoned it and, without losing his faith, decided to become a medical student. He went to study in Paris, became a hospital registrar and later head of a clinic. He was a kind, impressive, handsome man. In 1870 he met a young girl, with eyes like velvet and delicate features. He fell in love with her and they married. Jeanne Weil came from a Jewish family, originally from Lorraine, and had a considerable fortune. Her father, Nathée Weil, was a stockbroker; her uncle, Louis Weil, a confirmed bachelor, owned, in the rue La Fontaine, in Auteuil, what was considered in those days a suburban villa—a large house and garden where his niece took refuge to give birth, on the 10th July 1871, to her elder son: Marcel. Madame Proust's pregnancy, which coincided with the siege of Paris and the Commune, was a difficult one. It was for this reason that she had gone to stay with her uncle 'in the village of Auteuil'. Throughout his life, Marcel Proust retained a close link with his mother's family. As long as his health allowed, he went every year to visit the Weil family burying place. 'There is no one left'—he wrote sadly towards the end of his life 'not even I because I can't get up, to go to the little Jewish cemetery at the end of the rue du Repos where my grandfather, following a ritual the meaning of which he had never understood, went every year to place a pebble on his parents' grave. . . .' Such a duality of origin might well have inspired, at least at the outset, a natural agnosticism. Although Marcel Proust had been brought up in the Catholic faith and one might describe his whole work as a long striving towards a particular brand of mysticism, it does not seem that he was ever a believer. One of the few passages in which he gave some credit to the concept of the immortality of the soul is that wherein he describes the death of Bergotte and which ends with a question-mark, not with an affirmation.

But if Proust was not among those people who *know that it is true*, as Mauriac describes it, he showed from his earliest childhood a lively appreciation of the beauty of churches and of the poetry of religious ceremonies. With his brother, Robert, he used to go to the church of Illiers and place hawthorn on the altar of the Virgin Mary and this was the origin of his great love for 'that sweet, Catholic blossom'. In later years, he was never to see these pious flippant flowers without being reminded of an 'atmosphere of the bygone month of Mary, of Sunday afternoons, of faith and forgotten sins. . . .' His mother refused to be converted and all her life remained proudly, stubbornly devoted, if not to the Jewish faith, to the Jewish tradition, but his father was a practising Catholic and to the end of his days, Marcel remained aware of the virtues of Christianity. While he castigated the anti-semitism of certain priests who read *La Libre Parole*, he equally detested anticlericalism. In 1904, at the time of the Separation (between Church and State) he wrote a number of superb essays to defend 'the murdered churches' and he did this with his mother's approval.

The environment in which the child Proust developed was thus essentially a 'civilised' one. It was not only a combination of the lower middle class of Illiers and the upper middle class that stemmed from his family's material success: this usually means nothing and often produces, in other families, an awesome vulgarity. The atmosphere was permeated with a 'kind of unaffected aristocracy, without any titles . . . in which all social ambitions are justified because the habits and manners are in the best of traditions.' Doctor Adrien Proust contributed the gravity and the scientific mind that Marcel was to inherit; his mother gave him the love of literature, and a subtle sense of humour; it was she who was the first to mould the mind and taste of her son.

1871, and all that remained of the Salon de la Paix in Marie de' Medici's Tuileries Palace after the ravages of the Germans and the Commune. The vast edifice was later scavenged, the stones redressed and used for many of the buildings opposite on the left bank of the Seine.

In May, 1871, at the height of the Commune Dr Adrien Proust was nearly struck down by a stray bullet while walking in Paris. Despite the terrible bombardment of Auteuil by the government forces it seemed a safer place for the pregnant Jeanne Proust. Surrounded by the ruins she awaited the birth of her first born in her uncle Louis Weil's home.

The romanesque doorway is all that remains of the original eleventh century church of St Jacques. Inside, the memorials and blazonings of the ancient nobility of Illiers survive. Their histories and legends, their complicated genealogies were the well spring of the august lineage of the de Guermantes family.

'Tante Léonie's' house by van Dongen in the collection of Madame Mante-Proust, niece and heir of the author.

So many admirers of the book go to Illiers that the town has provided a guide map for the visitors.

The three-storied ancient building in the old rue Cheval-blanc with its rough-hewn arched doorway is where François Proust, Marcel's grandfather was born. Oncle Amiot's house still stands in the rue du Saint-Esprit, now renamed, in honour of his nephew, du Docteur Proust. The garden behind it has been maintained as it was, unlike the pâtisserie *which the young Marcel so loved, now a florist shop.*

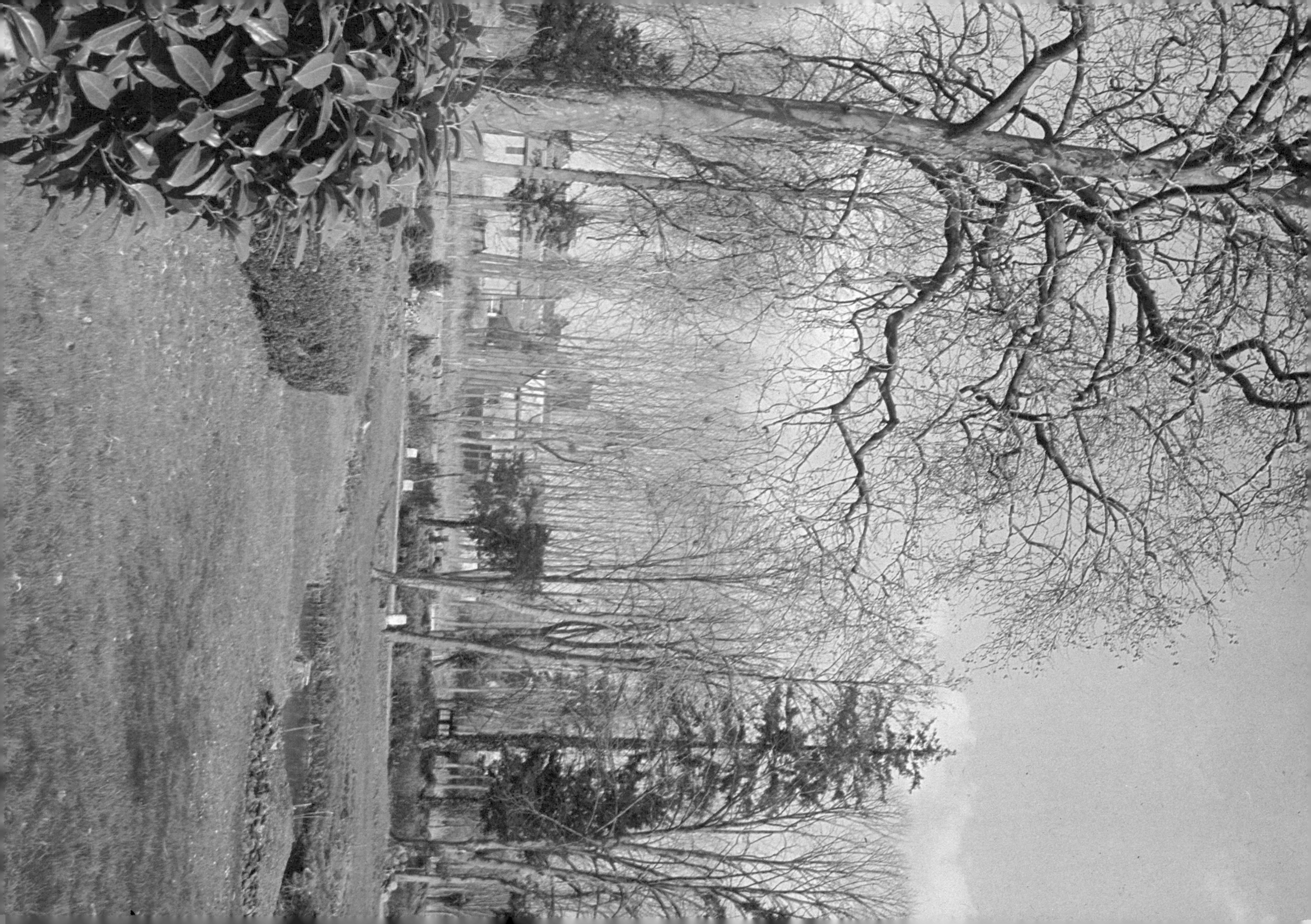

The view to the town from the Pré Catelan in which time would seem to have been trapped to remain faithful to the joy of the young narrator when he found himself in the early Easter time countryside, the trees not yet in full leaf, and the air a sweet secret to his happiness.

Beside the bank of one of the sources of the river Loir stands the ancient church of Saint Eman. In the book the river becomes the Vivonne, the church itself renamed St André des Champs, and from its real name came that of the Guermantes.

In March, *1871*, the government forces under Thiers removed the artillery from one of the outer defences to emplace them on the Butte de Montmartre and bomb the centre of Paris occupied by the Commune.

EPICERIE
Les défenseurs de la Commune. — Une femme conduisant une batterie de mitrailleuses place Taranne, le 22 mai
(Dessin de M. Sahib.)

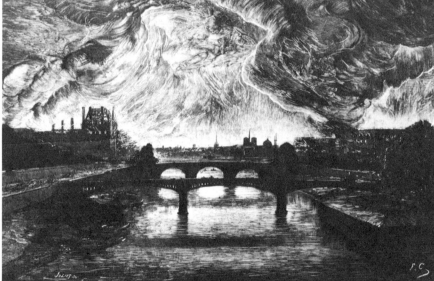

On 22 May a sympathetic woman led a group of machine gunners to a vantage point in the Place Tarrance. In that same month the Tuileries were fired spreading a cover of smoke and fire over the Seine.

In May, 1971, two months before the actual centenary of Proust's birthday a plaque was unveiled on the site, 96, rue de La Fontaine. The Society of the Friends of Marcel Proust and Combray, led by Madame Mante-Proust and

the president, André Brunet include Claude Gallimard, whose father was the first commercial publisher of A la recherche du temps perdu, *and Claude Mauriac.*

One of several photographs of the brothers Marcel and Robert taken in 1882 the year Marcel entered the Lycée Condorcet. Marcel's resemblance to his mother is remarkable.

Jeanne Proust's father Nathan Weil was a wealthy stock broker, just as was Swann's father. She was extremely well educated, spoke several languages and carefully supervised the education of her children.

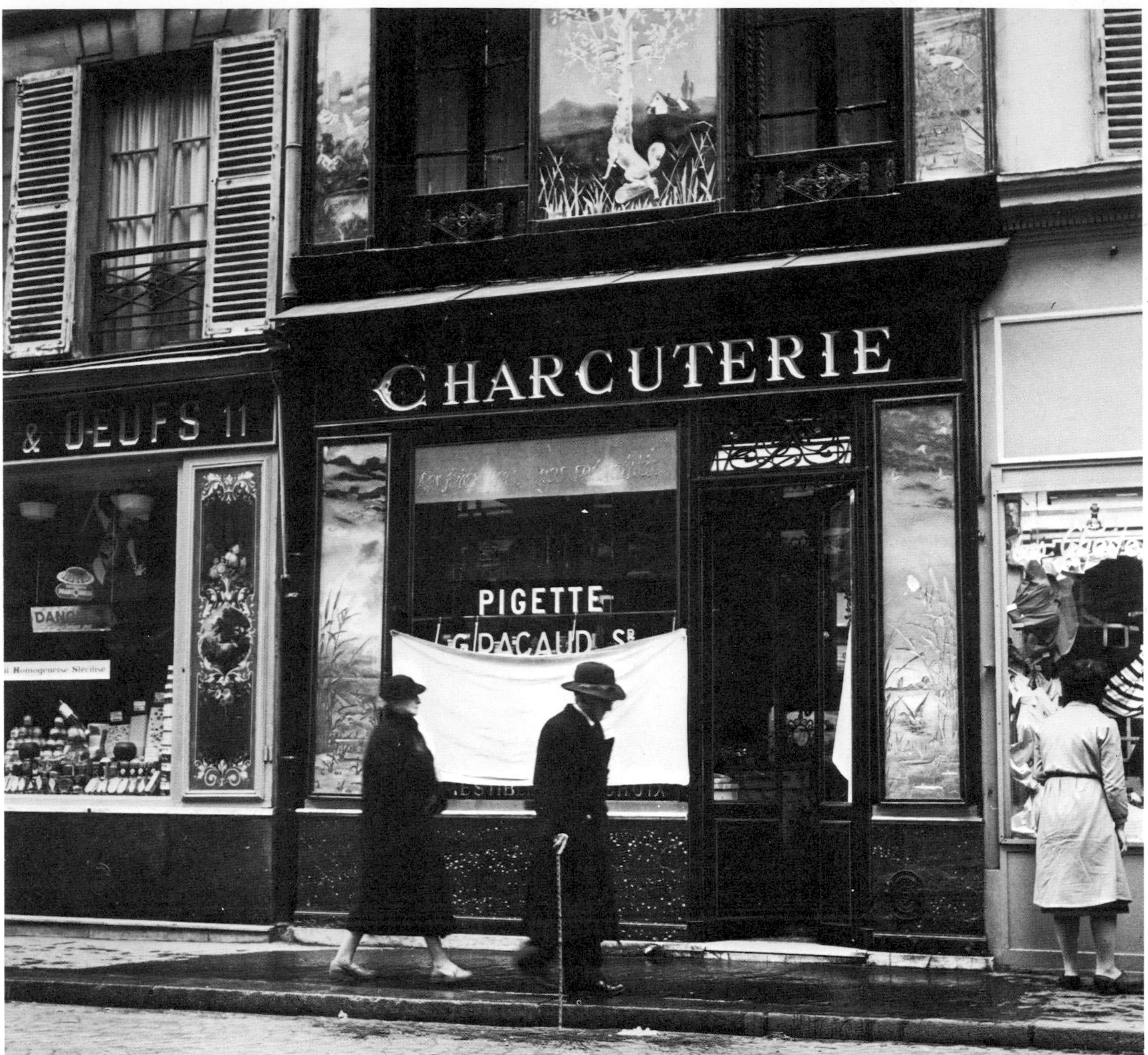

There can be found in Passy even today, in some of the corners and shop-fronts of that village-like part of Paris, places hardly changed since the Proust family moved there in 1882.

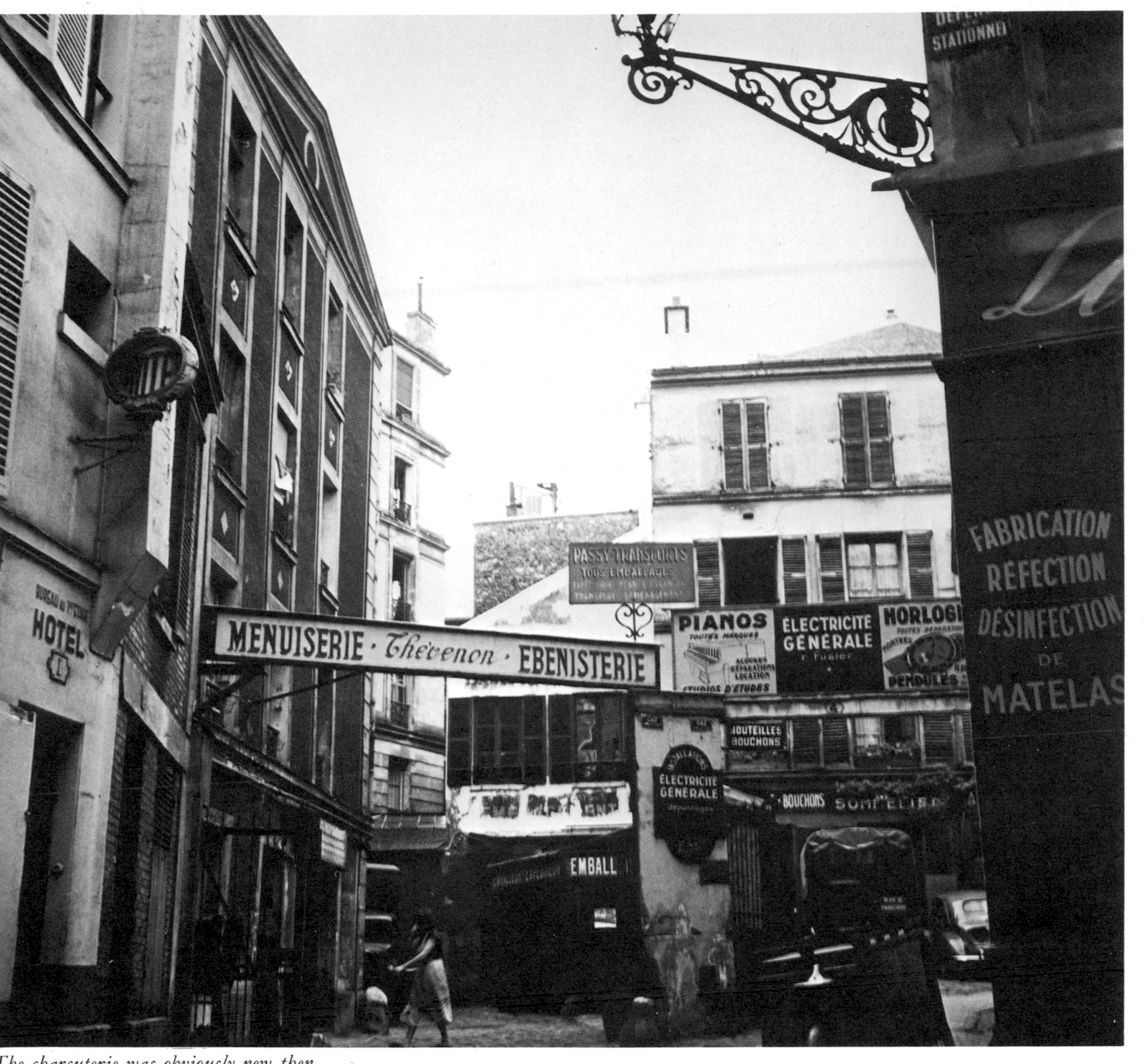

The charcuterie was obviously new then, and the conglomeration of various workshops if mostly for modern needs, still is essentially what it was like ninety years ago.

Upstream past houses with their backs sheltered towards the privacy only the great and noble could afford, Guermantes Way, in the young narrator's mind was this stretch of the Loir just outside Illiers.

Oncle Amiot and Tante Léonie in the little private park outside the town of Illiers which he created for himself and his family and named after Pré Catelan in the Bois de Boulogne.

The gardens were designed with palm trees, gravel paths and a small wandering stream wide enough to be leapt across. The water was planted with waterlilies and stocked well enough with carp for the children to fish for themselves.

But it was in the back gardens of the house on a summer evening in the rue du Saint-Esprit that the family would sit in garden chairs around a table laden with coffee.

From the time of his earliest reading, Proust became enamoured with the works of Balzac, and here is a curious link: few Parisians realise that at the corner of the rue Berton in Passy, this little precipitous impasse, rue Raynouard, is the house once inhabited by Balzac

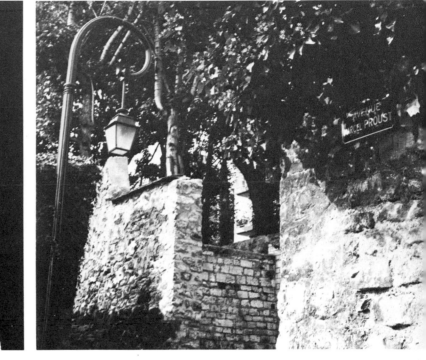

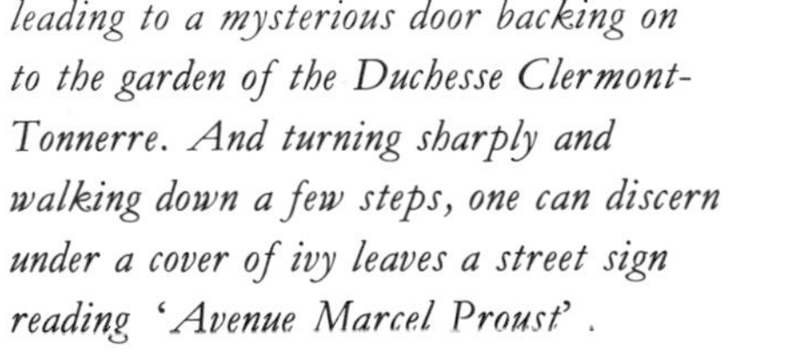
leading to a mysterious door backing on to the garden of the Duchesse Clermont-Tonnerre. And turning sharply and walking down a few steps, one can discern under a cover of ivy leaves a street sign reading 'Avenue Marcel Proust'.

224. TROUVILLE — Les Enfants s'amusent

Summer was not spent exclusively in Illiers. Towards the end of the season the family packed and set out for the Norman seaside be it Cabourg, Dieppe or Trouville.

Settings

Proust spent his childhood in four 'settings' which now, transformed and transposed by his artistry, we know so well. The first is Paris, where he lived with his parents, in a solid middle-class house, 9, Boulevard Malesherbes. In the afternoons he was taken to the Champs-Elysées, where, between the roundabouts and the laurel bushes beyond 'the frontier protected at equal distances by the bastions of the barley-sugar women', he played with a group of little girls who were later to become, all of them together, Gilberte. They were Marie and Nelly de Benardaky, Gabrielle Schwartz and Jeanne Pouquet (later, very much later, Princesse Radziwill, Comtesse de Contades, Madame L.-L. Klotz and Madame Gaston de Caillavet).

The second setting was Illiers, where the family spent their holidays at Tante Amiot's house at 4, rue du Saint-Esprit. What a joy it was, as soon as the train stopped, to run to the Loir and to find once again, according to the season, the hawthorns or the Easter buttercups, the poppies and the summer corn and always the old church with its hood of slate, dotted with crows, a shepherd watching his flock of houses. How he loved his room, with its long white curtains that concealed the bed, and the flowered counterpane, and embroidered quilt. He loved the glass trinity with the blue pattern that sat beside his bed, tumbler, carafe and sugar-bowl and on the mantelpiece the glass dome with the clock chattering beneath it; on the wall a print of the Saviour, and a twig of consecrated box. Above all, he loved the long hours spent reading in the 'Pré Catelan', in a small garden thus christened by Oncle Amiot to whom it belonged, a garden on the far bank of the Loir, enclosed by a particularly lovely hawthorn hedge, and at the end of which, in an arbour which still exists today, Marcel would drink in the deep silence, broken only by the golden chime of bells. It was there he read George Sand, Victor Hugo, Dickens, George Eliot and Balzac. 'There are perhaps no days in our childhood when we lived more fully than those which we believed to have passed without living them at all, the days that we spent with a favourite book. . . .'

The other settings were of lesser importance. There was the house of Oncle Weil in Auteuil, where 'Les Parisiens' took refuge on sultry days and which, in fact, contributed something towards the picture of the garden at Combray. Louis Weil was an old bachelor whose impenitent dissipation frequently shocked Marcel's conventional family and in whose house the child met pretty women who fondled him. Laure Hayman for example, the elegant demi-mondaine who was a descendant of an English painter [Francis Hayman], Gainsborough's master (and who contained some of the seeds that later germinated into the idea of Odette de Crécy).

Finally, for part of the summer, Marcel Proust was despatched with his grandmother to one or other of the Channel resorts, Trouville or Dieppe, and later Cabourg. Of such was born Balbec. In Madame Adrien Proust's diary we find 'Letter from my sweet Marcel, Cabourg, 9th September 1891. "How different from those years at the seaside when Grandmother and I, so perfectly at one together, used to talk as we battled against the wind." At one . . . never was a child so perfectly at one within a family so dearly loved. . . .' One can find great pleasure in making pilgrimages to the places that have served as frameworks and models for the great masterpieces, to search in Saumur or Guérande for what Balzac saw there, in Combourg for the melancholy evenings that Chateaubriand described, in Illiers for the hawthorn and the reeds of the Vivonne. Confrontations of this kind, however, not only fail to conjure up for us the vivid images born of the writer's magic, they bring home to us the immense gap that separates the model from the work of art. 'If we needed proof that there is not only one world, but as many worlds as there are individuals and all different, what could prove it more conclusively than the fact that when we see, in someone's collection, a barn, a church, a farm or a tree, we say to one another: "Look: an Elstir!" recognising in them fragments of a world that Elstir saw and that only he could see.' Thus Proust saw 'Prousts' in all the landscapes of his childhood and just as Renoir touched all flesh with the rainbow of his palette, so Marcel hung his lovely garlands of rare adjectives about the trees of La Beauce and the Champs-Elysées alike. This beauty, however, remains his own and those who only see in nature what exists in reality will, without doubt, be disappointed when they try to recapture there the soft sheen and the velvet of his epithets.

Proust said himself how disappointing it would be to visit the places which had seemed so enchanting to readers of Maeterlinck and Anna de Noailles. 'We would like to search out the field that Millet shows us in his *Spring* (for painters teach us in the manner of the poets); we would like to have Claude Monet for our guide to Giverny, on the banks of the Seine and to that bend in the river he barely allows us to glimpse in the morning mist. In reality, however, it was only the purest chance of having relations or parents who provide the opportunity of visiting or staying with them, that decided Madame de Noailles, Maeterlinck, Millet or Claude Monet to choose to put on paper this road, this garden, this field or this particular bend in the river rather than any other.' The enchanted garden that Proust described where he sat reading undiscovered in an arbour in sight of the white gate that marked 'the end of the parkland' and beyond which lay the fields of cornflowers and poppies, this garden was not simply the Pré Catelan at Illiers—no, we have all known it and all lost it, for it existed only because we were young, and in our imaginations.

Even in the back garden of Tante Léonie's there was refuge and a place to dream and hope for anticipated pleasures and try to put away doubts.

Swann's Way: Tansonville, the name given to Swann's great house and park come from this small château, whereas the lovely house Roussainville gave its name to the ruined keep the narrator enjoyed for his secret pleasure.

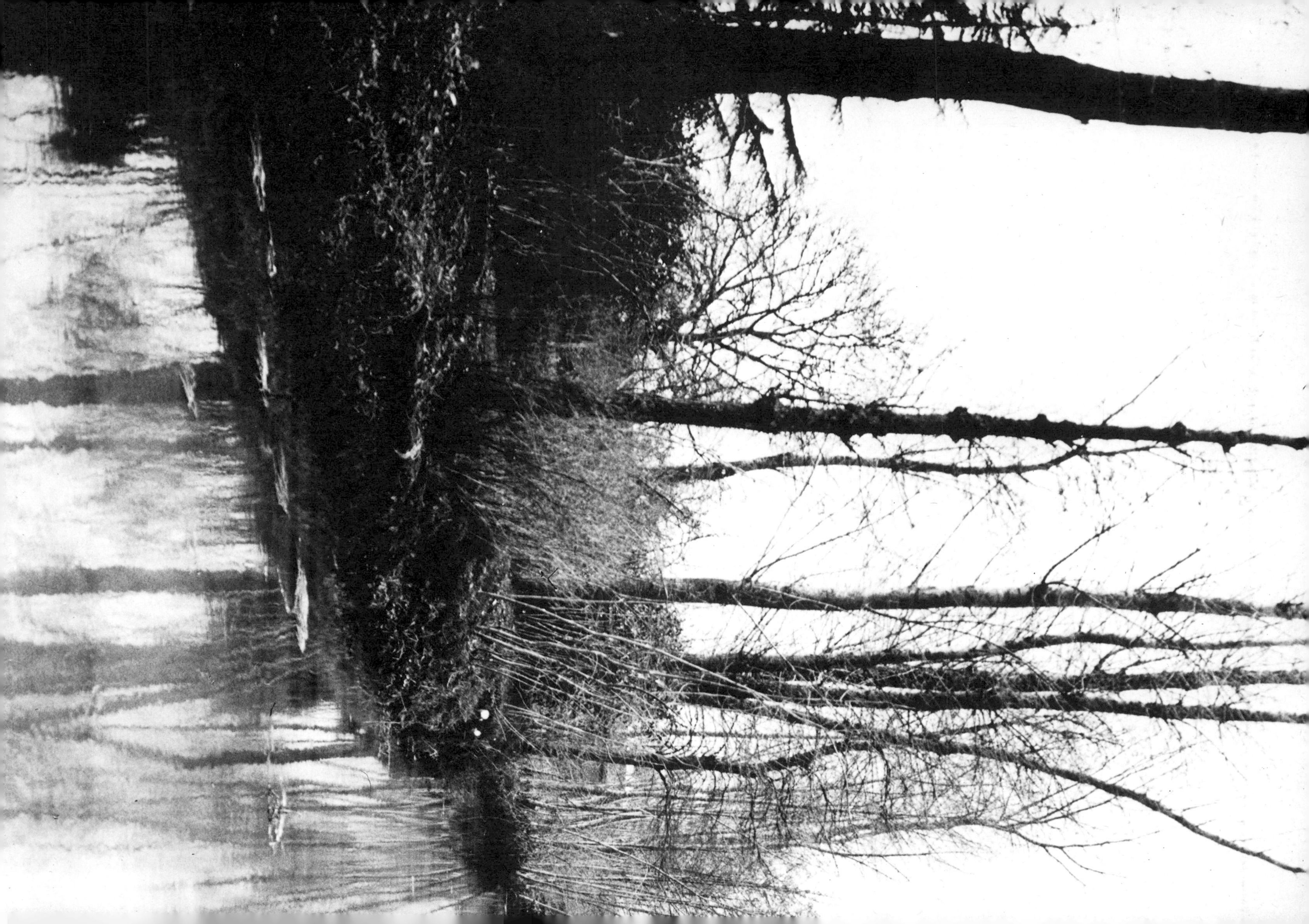

Pont St Hilaire bridges the Loir leading to the ruined church whose name was substituted for that of St Jacques. The ruined towers at the end of the promenade de la Citadelle were the hiding place of the young Marcel.

The park Monceau's grillework leads into the elaborate classical garden which has always echoed with the sounds of children at play or confiding to one another, in his time and today.

Within the park Monceau young Marcel, an unidentified friend and Antoinette Faure, one of the several models whose characteristics are combined to create Gilberte.

Madame Jeanne Proust

Dr Adrien Proust

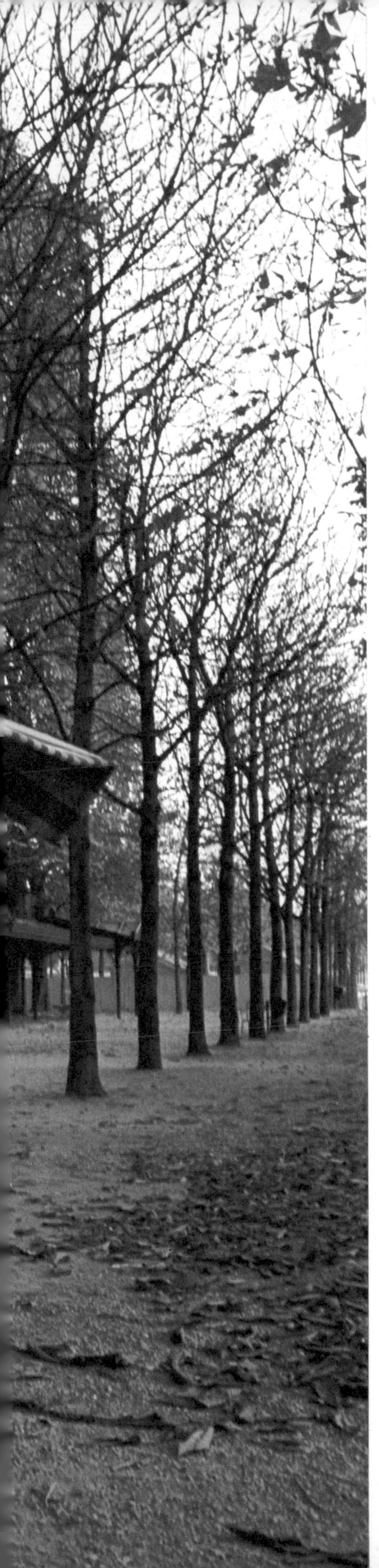

Champs-Elysée kiosk: 1972, 1883

Crossing from in front of the Elysée palace on the northern side of the Champs-Elysée is a small path leading diagonally to the Champs, roughly the route the young narrator and his friends took to the kiosk. Grandmother's near fatal heart attack was in this châlet de nécessité.

The Boy

Despite poor health and his attacks of asthma, Marcel Proust had a normal education, indeed a very sucessful one, at the Lycée Condorcet where literature was held in high esteem, that is to say, literature not of the elaborate, classical style of the Lycées of Louis-le-Grand or Henri IV, but rather of the modern, precious and decadent school. A kind of clique came into being at Condorcet that cut across several classes of boys of good family who were all besotted with literature: Daniel Halévy, Fernand Gregh, Marcel Proust, Jacques Bizet, Robert de Flers, Jacques Baignères, Robert Dreyfus, Louis de la Salle, Marcel Boulenger, Gabriel Trarieux. By 1888 there was in Condorcet a circle whose attraction was so strong that certain pupils, of whom Proust was one, used to come to school early so they could meet and discuss 'in the scanty shade of the trees that lined the Cour du Havre, as they waited for the drum roll that advised, rather than commanded, them to go in to class.'

What did they read? They read anything that was considered 'modern': Barrès, France, Lemaître, Maeterlinck. They decided that Léon Dierx and Leconte de Lisle, too esoteric for earlier generations, were 'difficult' poets. Marcel Proust shared these tastes and remained faithful to them for a long time: not to admire Maeterlinck was one of the absurdities of the Duchesse de Guermantes. Thanks to his mother, however, he had long been familiar with the classics, with an especial predilection for Saint-Simon, La Bruyère, Madame de Sévigné, Musset, George Sand, Baudelaire. He was an avid reader of *The Arabian Nights* and, in translation, of Dickens, Thomas Hardy, Stevenson and George Eliot. 'Two pages of *The Mill on the Floss* and I weep. . . .' The philosophy year (1888–1889) was for Proust the year of his greatest intellectual enrichment. This was the period when 'a kind of imminent immaterialism' was succeeding the materialism of Taine and Berthelot, when Alain found Lagneau's lectures on Plato and Spinoza as clear as black ink on white paper.

Lachelier, Fouillée and Boutroux were preparing the ground for Bergson. Proust was lucky enough to have Professor Darlu as his teacher. ('A fine brain' Anatole Francc said of him, a compliment which might have seemed a trifle guarded had not Darlu said precisely the same of France.) This warm-hearted, sarcastic and stimulating southerner was, according to Fernand Gregh, like a conjurer, and used to bring his philosophy out of his top hat which he was inclined to leave on his lectern and use when he needed an object for his demonstrations.

'Conception of a sick mind . . . Sganarelle's philosophy'—was the kind of comment Darlu made on an essay, in this case an essay by one of the brightest pupils in the class. On Proust, however, he had a profound and permanent influence. In his lectures on the reality of the exterior world, he had a poetical approach to his subject which later allowed Proust 'to incorporate into the novel a whole world of thought and even a style which hitherto had belonged only to philosophers.' Later Proust studied Renouvier,

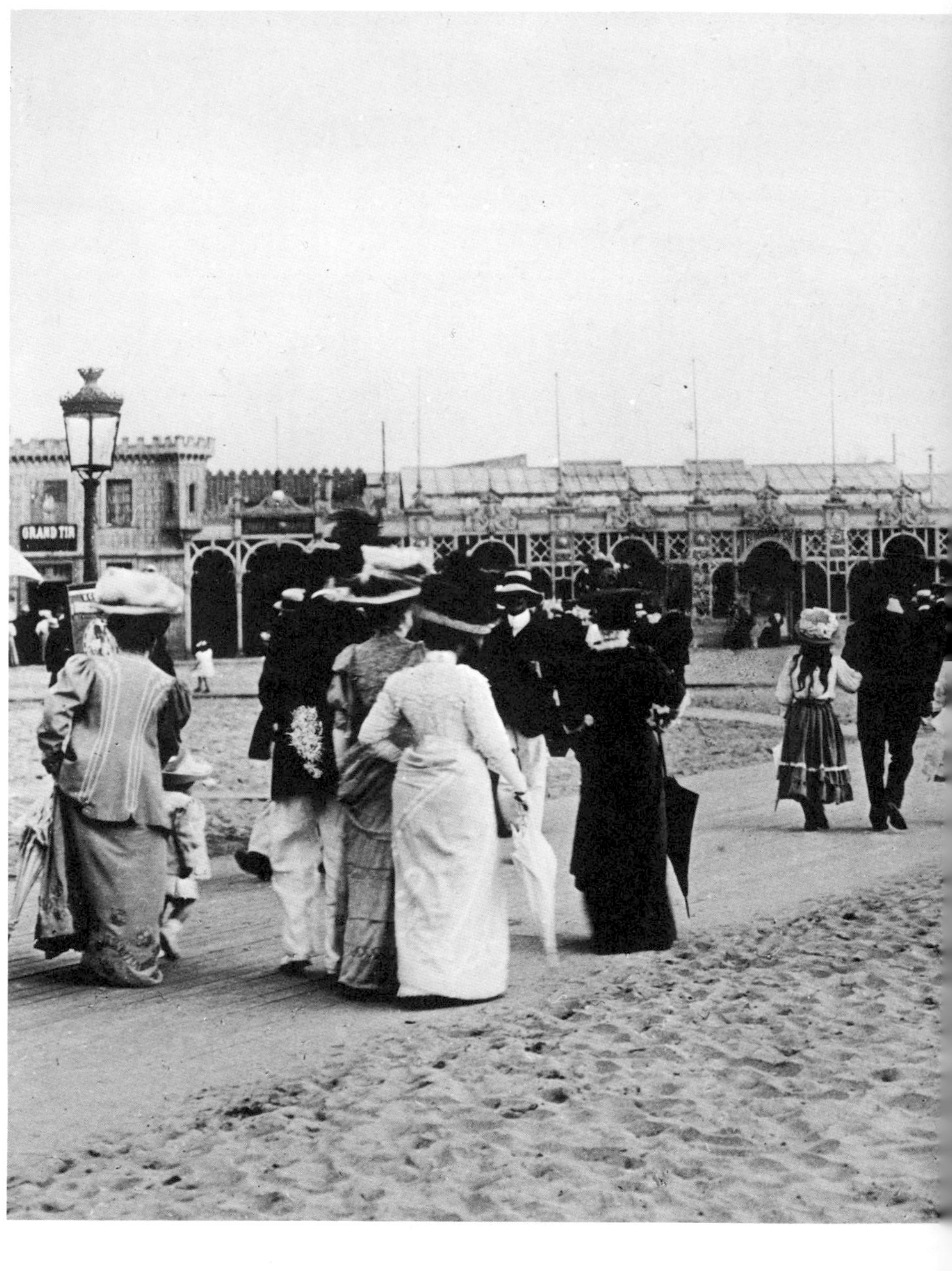

Trouville at the height of the season where as a boy and frequently in manhood Proust sought the sea air as a relief to his chronic asthma. The boyhood playground later became the scene of summer social calls to the houses of friends with dinners, musicales, days at the races, or searching out the countryside for medieval ruins.

Boutroux and Bergson, but he always maintained that Darlu was the great teacher of his life and it was Darlu who paved the way for that long meditation on the unreality of the perceptible world, on Memory and on Time, which is for us *La recherche du temps perdu*.

Close as was the relationship between mother and son, their lives soon took different directions. Madame Adrien Proust did not care for Society and, besides, knew very little of it. In her case the Prousts of Illiers had meant no more than the addition of a provincial family to her own Hebrew stock. Doctor Proust, who was becoming one of the high priests of public medicine, dreamed of being elected to the Académie des Sciences Morales and was

inclined to cultivate friendships that might be useful to him, but his wife often preferred that he went out alone. On grand occasions, his two sons used to watch with admiration as he fixed the red ribbon of a Commandeur de la Légion d'Honneur under his white tie. Since his adolescence Marcel had shown a taste for Society that amounted almost to a craving. Some of his friends at Condorcet—Jacques Baignères, Gaston de Caillavet, for example—had young mothers who entertained a great deal. At one of their houses, he made the acquaintance of Madeleine Lemaire whose studio had, at that time, become a 'salon'. His friend Jacques Bizet had introduced him to his mother, née Geneviève Halévy, daughter of Fromental Halévy, who composed *La Juive*, and widow of the

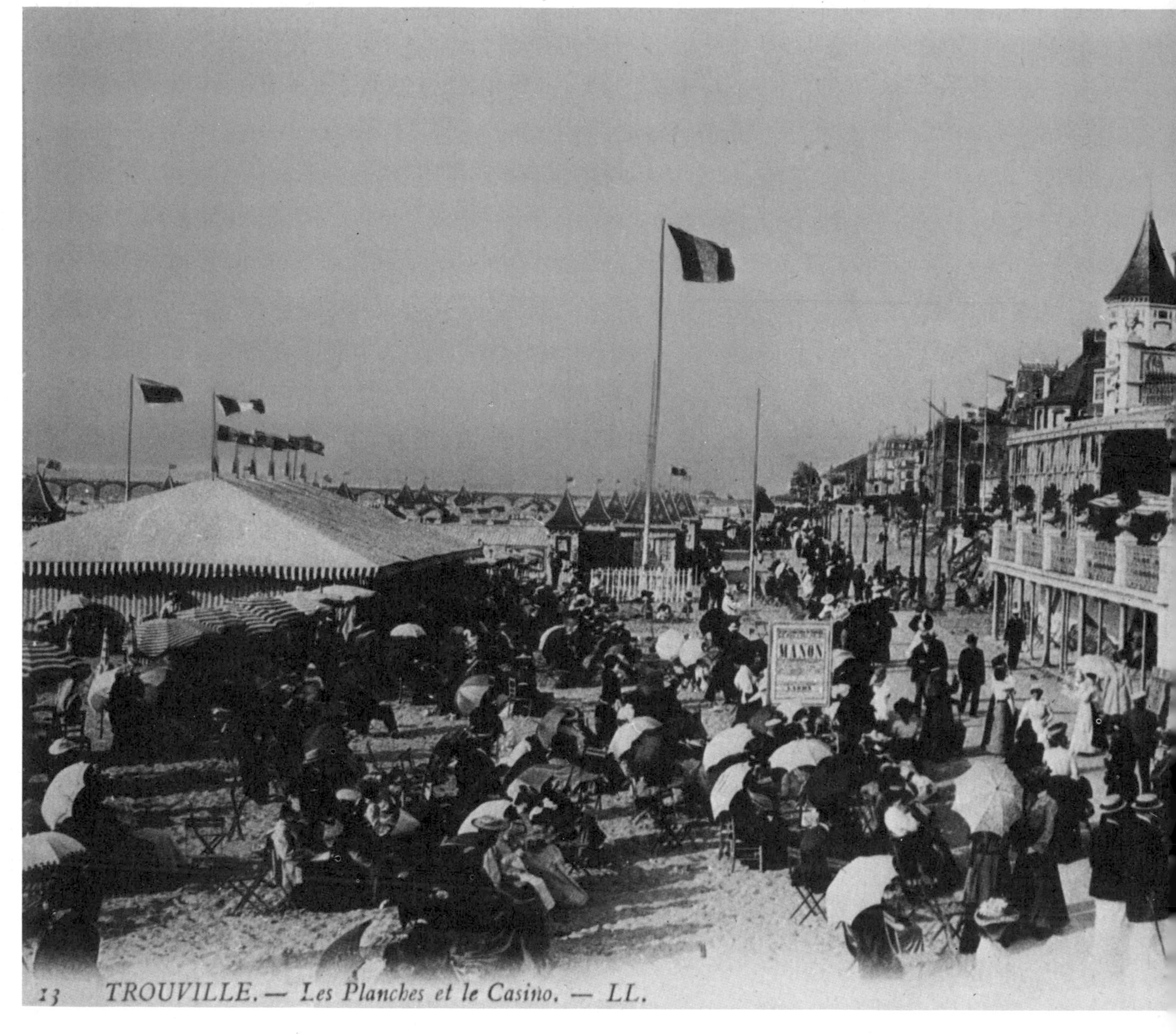

13 TROUVILLE. — *Les Planches et le Casino.* — LL.

composer of *Carmen*, and who had now married a rich lawyer, Emile Straus. At 43 Madame Straus was still beautiful, with the warm, brown eyes of a gypsy and 'a primitive, oriental and melancholy grace'. She was not a women of great culture, but Proust was drawn to her by her charm, her whims, her wit and by her letters which he rashly compared to those of Madame de Sévigné. To Madame Straus, Marcel Proust, schoolboy, paid respectful and symbolic court. He besieged her with flowers, both literally and figuratively, and would then implore her not to think he loved her any less simply because, for several days, he had not been able to send her any chrysanthemums. 'But Mademoiselle Lemaire can tell you that I walk every morning with Laure Hayman and often

take her to luncheon, and that costs me such a lot I've nothing left for flowers . . . and, apart from a few sous' worth of poppies for Madame Lemaire, I don't think I've sent flowers to anyone since I sent them last to you. . . .' For a long time he continued to lavish on her protestations of eternal devotion: 'Madame, if there is anything that I can do to give you pleasure, take a letter for you to Stockholm or to Naples or anything else you can think of, that would make me very, very happy. . . .' Laure Hayman, 'a strange courtesan with a touch of affectation about her, doted on her young Proust and trailed him everywhere after her, calling him 'mon petit Marcel' or 'mon petit Saxe psychologique'. When Paul Bourget made her the heroine of *Gladys Harvey* she sent a copy of

The town life of Trouville's summer residents centred on the hotels, the casino, the promenade and the quay. Behind the fashionable facade, the old town, largely built on 17th and 18th century slums furnished the summer residents with the necessary supplies of food and service. The harbour always has been, unlike so many society resorts, a working port for the Norman fishermen.

Le Petit
Journal

Deauville in summer: changes in fashion and the growth of the trees and modes of traffic are the perceptible differences between 1900, 1922 and 1958.

But in Illiers there was always Oncle Amiot's Prè-Catelan entrance (below) and the pavilion in which to read or watch a world limited by the double gates at the end of the park.

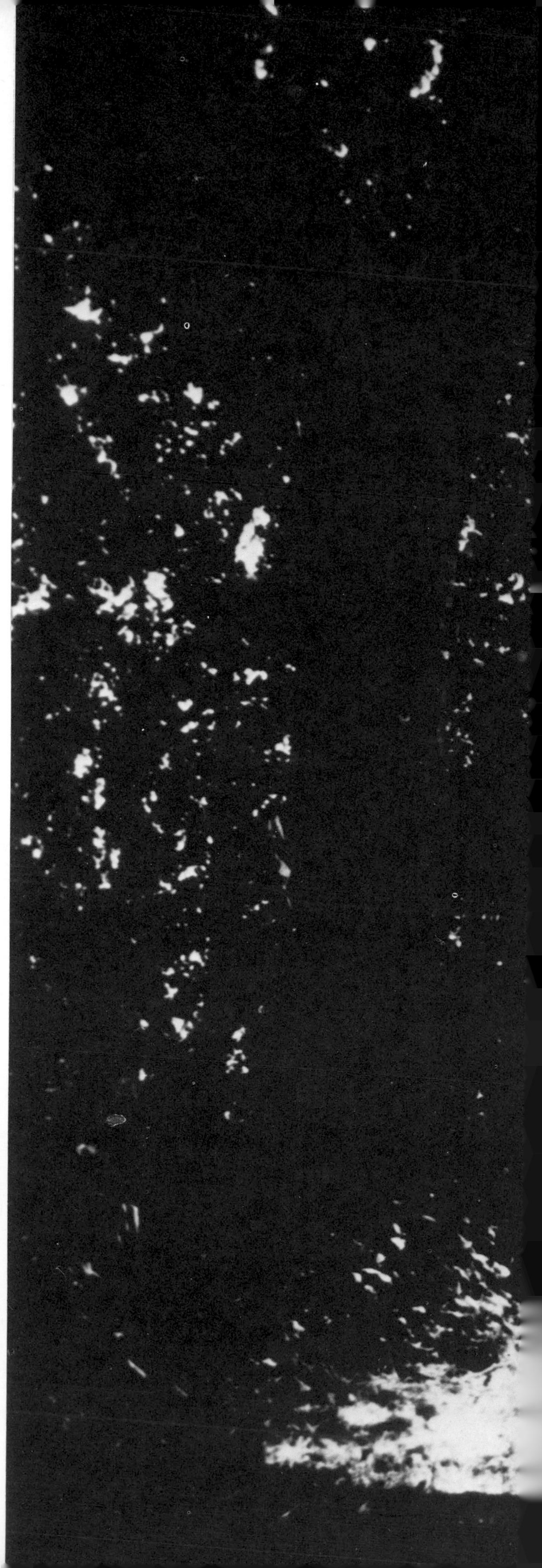

the book to Marcel, wrapped up in the flowered silk of one of her petticoats. What a strange boy he must have been! Like the Narrator in his book, he seems to have had no precise age. Was he child? Or adolescent? It would be hard to tell. 'There was much more in him of the schoolboy he had ceased to be than of the dandy which was what he longed to be. Marcel had been very much the Condorcet student, with his flower in his buttonhole and his wing collars. Later he wore pale green ties, knotted anyhow, baggy trousers and a flowing frock-coat. He would twirl his malacca cane as he retrieved a soiled and crumpled pearl grey glove—beaded in black—that he would let fall while pulling on or taking off its

In those days the students of the ancient Lycée Condorcet were escorted and met by their parents. Today the boys make their own way.

partner. Marcel left these odd gloves all over the place and then would beg you to return a missing one in an envelope, in return for a new pair or half a dozen new pairs which he would present to you in gratitude for its restoration. It was the same with his umbrellas, which he shed in cabs and in the halls of friends' houses; the most dilapidated ones he would continue to carry if you returned them promptly, but he would always buy you a new one at Verdier's. As for his top hats, they came to resemble hedgehogs and skye-terriers from being too often brushed the wrong way and rubbed against skirts and furs in carriages—and the majority of them came from Binder's. . . .'

In the portrait that Blanche painted of him, we see a head a trifle on the large side, splendid eyes 'a liquid eye with brown and golden lights'. It had a haunting look to it in which sadness acquired from the summing up of the world mingled with a lively malice, and where indifference, which he suddenly wanted complete, reflected the shining spark of fervour, of dreams and infinite perspectives!; a mass of black hair that was always untidy, a necktie a shade too bright, an orchid in his buttonhole, a mixture of indolence and of the dandy that very fleetingly recalled the figure of Oscar Wilde. 'A Neapolitan prince in a novel by Bourget,' said Fernand Gregh.

Of all his teachers at the Lycée it was Alphonse Darlu (first row, second from the right) who had the greatest influence on the student. It was his inspired talks, Proust later wrote, which were more lasting than anything written, which brought forth in him and in so many others the power to think.

Meetings

He joined the army in 1889, without waiting to be called up, in order to take advantage of the 'volunteer' scheme, then in its last year, whereby he was only obliged to complete one year's military service. He was sent to Orléans, to the 76th infantry regiment, and thanks to an 'intelligent' colonel, that is to say, a colonel sensitive to the prestige of civilian rank and open to letters of recommendation, he did not suffer unduly from the disparity between barracks and home. A rather pathetic portrait shows him as a shabby footslogger in an ill-fitting greatcoat with his beautiful Persian prince's eyes lost beneath the peak of a flowerpot képi. To Robert de Billy, future ambassador, who was in the artillery at Orléans at the time, Proust's bearing and his conversation were about as unmilitary as they could be: 'He had great questioning eyes and spoke in a friendly, relaxed fashion. He talked to me about Monsieur Darlu, his professor of philosophy at Condorcet, and the novel thoughts which emanated from this Lycée on the right bank seemed to me, for I had only been a maths scholar at the Bazar Louis, of a modernity that was perhaps contemptible but, who knows, might well have been sublime. . . .' In the training platoon, Proust came 63rd out of 64. The good pupil was not a brilliant soldier. He spent his Sunday 'pass' in Paris, delighted to rejoin his friends. He was to visit Madame Arman de Caillavet, a formidable hostess, and the Egérie of Anatole France whose son, Gaston, had become one of Marcel's closest friends and who carried his 'sweetness' to the length of taking him to the train to Orléans every Sunday evening. *Marcel Proust to Jeanne Pouquet*: 'If you recall that, at that time, there were no taxis, you'll be amazed to think that each time I returned to Orléans on the 7.40 train, he drove me to the station . . . and once he even came all the way to Orléans. I had an enormous affection for Gaston; in the barracks I talked of no-one else until my corporal and my batman and various others began to think him some kind of god. On New Year's Day they sent him an address 'as a mark of respect.' It was at Madame de Caillavet's house that Proust met Anatole France whose style he admired and who was to supply him with several features for the character of Bergotte. He had always imagined France to be a 'sweet songster with snow-white hair'; when he came face to face with this man with a nose like a 'snail's shell', a little black beard and a slight stammer, he was very disappointed. The Anatole France he had 'built up, drop by drop, like a stalactite, from the transparent beauty of his books was no more use to him once he had to accept the "snail's-shell" nose and the little black beard.' Nose and beard forced him to 'build up the character all over again'; he was distressed to have 'to attach this bearded gentleman to the original image, as to a balloon,' without being sure that the balloon would rise. 'You who care so much for the things of the mind . . .' France said to him. 'I don't at all care for the things of the mind; I only care for life and for movement,' Proust replied. He was sincere: intelligence came so naturally to him that he placed no value on its workings, whereas he both envied and admired the grace of people who lived instinctively. When he came out of the army, he would have liked to have gone on with his studies. Since childhood, there had only been one career for him and that was writing; from very early on he had known that a writer's discipline was, of necessity, exhausting and exclusive. He adored his parents, however, and could not bear to cross them. It was Doctor Proust's wish that he should enter the diplomatic service. Since filial respect condemned him to waste his time, and as the route to the embassies lay by way of the *Ecole des Sciences Politiques*, he decided to go there. And here he met up again with Robert de Billy and Gabriel Trarieux and, with them, attended the lectures of Albert Sorel, Albert Vandal and Leroy-Beaulieu. He listened carefully, took no notes and wrote in a virgin exercise-book:

Vandal exquis répand son sel,
Mais qui s'en fout, c'est Gabriel,
Robert, Jean et même Marcel,
Pourtant si grave d'habitude.

Proust volunteered for a year of military service and joined the 76th Infantry at Orleans, 15 November 1889. Among his officers was a Capitaine Waleweski, who, like his father, bore a strong resemblance to Napoleon and appears in the Guermantes Way as Capitaine Prince de Borodino.

113 ORLEANS.
Caserne du Quartier Châtillon (Artillerie). — ND Ph
ANCIENN! Qr de BEL-AIR

Was he so serious? He was indeed serious but he was frivolous also—which is not a contradiction in terms. 'Frivolity is an extreme state of mind.' He loved going to tennis parties at the boulevard Bineau at Neuilly, with Gaston de Caillavet and his friends. His poor health would not allow him to play but his talent for conversation would attract around him under the trees a circle of young girls and mothers who were still young. As he was put in charge of the food, he always arrived bearing an enormous box of delicacies. If it was very warm they would despatch him to a nearby bistro in search of beer and lemonade which, moaning and groaning, he would carry back in a terrible basket borrowed from the proprietor. Sometimes a ball would alight in the middle of the petits fours, scattering glasses and young women. Marcel would always accuse the players of having aimed 'with malice and without cause'. Perhaps there may have been a cause of which the guilty ones themselves were unconscious. Marcel's charm, his sensitivity and his vitality very often exasperated his friends; they were a little jealous of him and without being aware of harbouring any ill-feeling towards him, they were not perhaps reluctant to interrupt 'the Court of Love' which was what they called 'the gossip circle' when in poetic vein. When the game was over the players would come and rest in the shade 'of the budding grove' and join the young women listening to Marcel. Many years later, when he was writing one of his books, he recalled those days and wrote to Jeanne Pouquet (by this time married to Gaston de Caillavet): 'You will find woven into it some of that emotion I used to feel when I asked myself if you were going to be at the tennis party? But what is the good of remembering things which you took such an absurd and malicious delight in pretending not to notice? . . .' He went on with his studies, but without enthusiasm. Professor Proust and his wife were too fond of him to wish to bring any permanent pressure to bear on their son. They were in despair when Marcel, who had enrolled in the Faculty of Law, failed the second part of his examinations. Finally, his parents gave him permission to attend lectures at the Sorbonne, without any particular aim in view, which was what he had always wanted. It was there that he studied under Henri Bergson, now related to him by his marriage with Mademoiselle Neuburger, and who, like Darlu, believed in the vital alliance of poetry and philosophy. On the surface, the four or five years that followed his military service were further wasted years for Marcel; in fact, like a bee gathering honey, he was filling his hive with personalities and impressions. Around him, in the literary and poetical worlds, all kinds of schools of thought and parties were springing up; nationalism and symbolism were fighting over the rising generation. Marcel Proust, however, was not remotely interested in such movements. Just as, at Illiers he had laid in a store of impressions of nature, now in Paris he was trying to analyse and understand creative art. Some of his friends were able to initiate him into the world of painting, and they made long expeditions to the Louvre; through others, he discovered music. There were many who reproached him for being too much attracted towards the Faubourg Saint-Germain. This was partly, says Fernand Gregh, because it represented a world that was beyond his reach. Why did he, in later years, so obviously enjoy describing the brilliant social career of a man like Swann? It was because Swann's career resembled his own, and because, in both cases, the prestige that taste and intelligence bestow were able to overcome hostility and prejudice. It is true that he wrote once to Paul Souday that it had been difficult for a man like himself, who had always lived in that world, to put himself in the shoes of a Narrator who knew no duchesses and who longed to know them, but this is one of the rare occasions when he permits himself, consciously or unconsciously, to be inaccurate. His conquest of society began early, it is true, but it was indeed a conquest and he had had to fight for it.

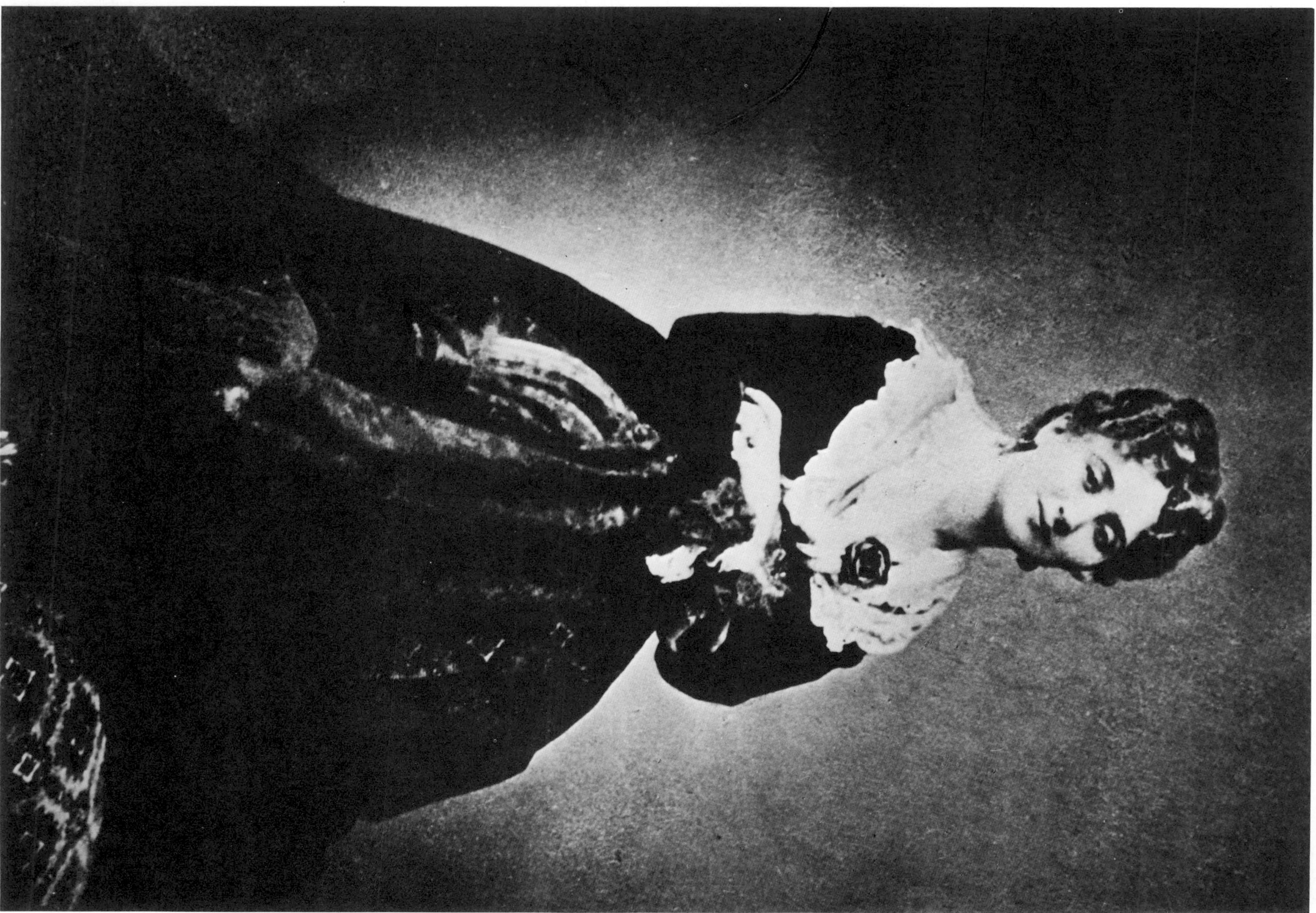

Madame Arman de Caillavet, many of whose idiosyncracies are recognisable in Madame Verdurin, was one of several ferocious literary hostesses. The principal ornament of her salon was Anatole France (the model for Bergotte) with whom, despite the presence of her husband, she had an all but acknowledged liaison. The writer spent almost all his time at her house and shared their meals. The days began by making love in his bachelor flat, then to her apartment for lunch, and at teatime the drawing-room door would open with France saying 'I happened to be in the neighbourhood and felt I had to pay my respects' . Gaston de Caillavet, her son, is one of the people who go into the make-up of St Loup.

Relationships

The campaign began with the hostesses of his adolescence: Madame Straus, Madame Henri Baignères, her sister-in-law Madame Arthur Baignères (nicknamed the 'Unguarded Tower'), Madame Arman de Caillavet and also Madeleine Lemaire, a water-colourist 'who has created more roses than anyone after God', in whose drawing-room Proust met the Princesse Mathilde, and where for the first time he saw the Comtesse Greffulhe and Madame de Chevigné, his future models. It was there that he formed a close friendship with the musician, Reynaldo Hahn, 'who had all the

Laure Hayman, who was for a while Oncle Louis Weil's acknowledged mistress was one of the more intelligent and thoughtful of the 'grandes horizontales' of her day. Her lovers were invariably noble and some princely. She never ruined any of them financially and was named "the educator of dukes" for her attention to the arts of literature, manners and love. More than a little of her life is to be found in Odette de Crécy.

virtues to excess and was the master of all the charms'. Three years younger than Marcel, born in Venezuela but of the culture that was entirely French, Reynaldo displayed a precocious talent, exquisite taste and a curiously universal intelligence. Whether he was sitting playing or singing at the piano, or talking about books or people, there was something at once tender and mercurial about the way he improvised, that was quite unique. 'I like the way you sing,' Pauline Viardot said to him one day—'Yes, it's simple and it's true. . . .' And in the same way, his friends liked the way he talked.

By their deep and demanding devotion to art, their common loathing of emphasis and the real seriousness behind their feigned frivolities, Marcel Proust and Reynaldo Hahn were born to be friends. It was Reynaldo more than anyone else who helped Marcel to understand music and who gathered together for him the

One of the many photographs taken in Madame Straus' mulberry garden. They met when Proust was a fellow schoolboy of Jacques Bizet, her son by Georges Bizet.

elements that were to become 'Vinteuil's little phrase'. Passionate friends, they read the great masterpieces together: Marcus Aurelius, the *Mémoires d'Outre-Tombe*, and worshipped the nobility they discovered there. Marcel prized Reynaldo's innate awareness of literary beauty; Reynaldo admired Marcel for knowing instinctively that, in Duparc's *Invitation au Voyage,* the music 'Mon enfant, ma soeur' was vastly overwritten. They had the same love of nature, the same melancholy pessimism. On this perfect community of tastes was built a friendship which was to make them inseparable for many years. In 1893, at the house of Madeleine Lemaire, Proust met Comte Robert de Montesquiou, gentleman poet (then aged thirty-eight), 'whose airs and graces had many disciples and whose very arrogance was captivating'. An aesthete 'who was both absurd and fascinating, half musketeer, half prelate' and who was believed to have been the inspiration of Huysmans' *Des*

Luncheon in the country with friends of the family. Proust stands to the right of his mother, and Dr Proust is seated to the right.

Comte Robert de Billy and Proust met when they were both doing their military service and later together attended the College of Political Science. They went to the same salons and through the years remained fast friends and confidants.

Esseintes, Montesquiou indulged, in his verse and in his bibelots, in all the contortions of the 'fin de siècle' style. 'His impeccably gloved hands made beautiful gestures and even the flick of his wrists was harmonious.' Sometimes he would remove his gloves and raise an exquisite hand to the heavens. He wore a solitary ring, simple and exotic at the same time, on his finger. 'As he raised his hand, so his voice would rise with it, till it blared like a trumpet in an orchestra, and then would fall again plaintive and weeping, while his forehead wrinkled and his eyebrows drew together to form a tight little circumflex accent. . . .' At their very first meeting, Proust saw how useful such a man might be, both to his career in society and to his work, and immediately he was signing himself

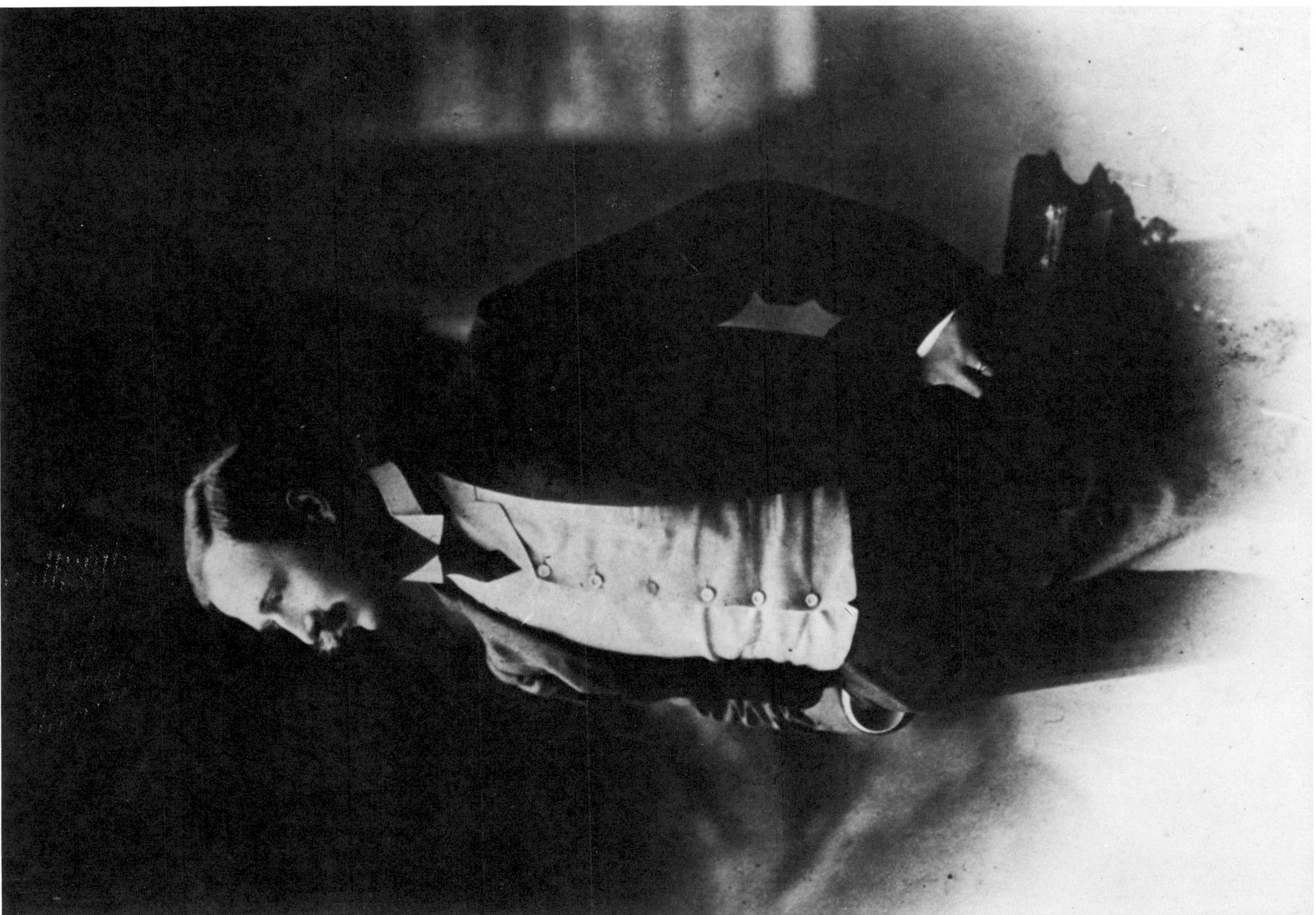

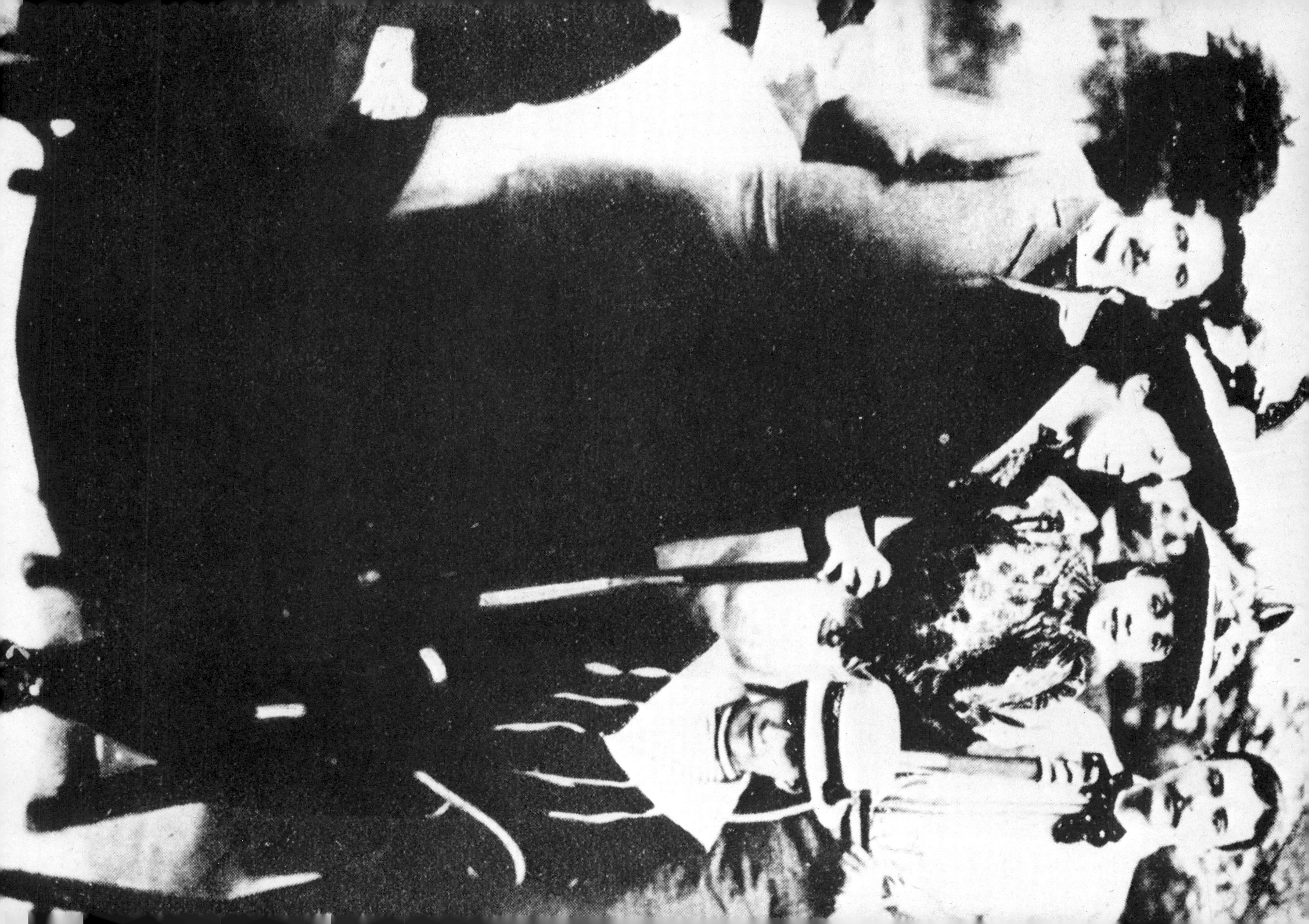

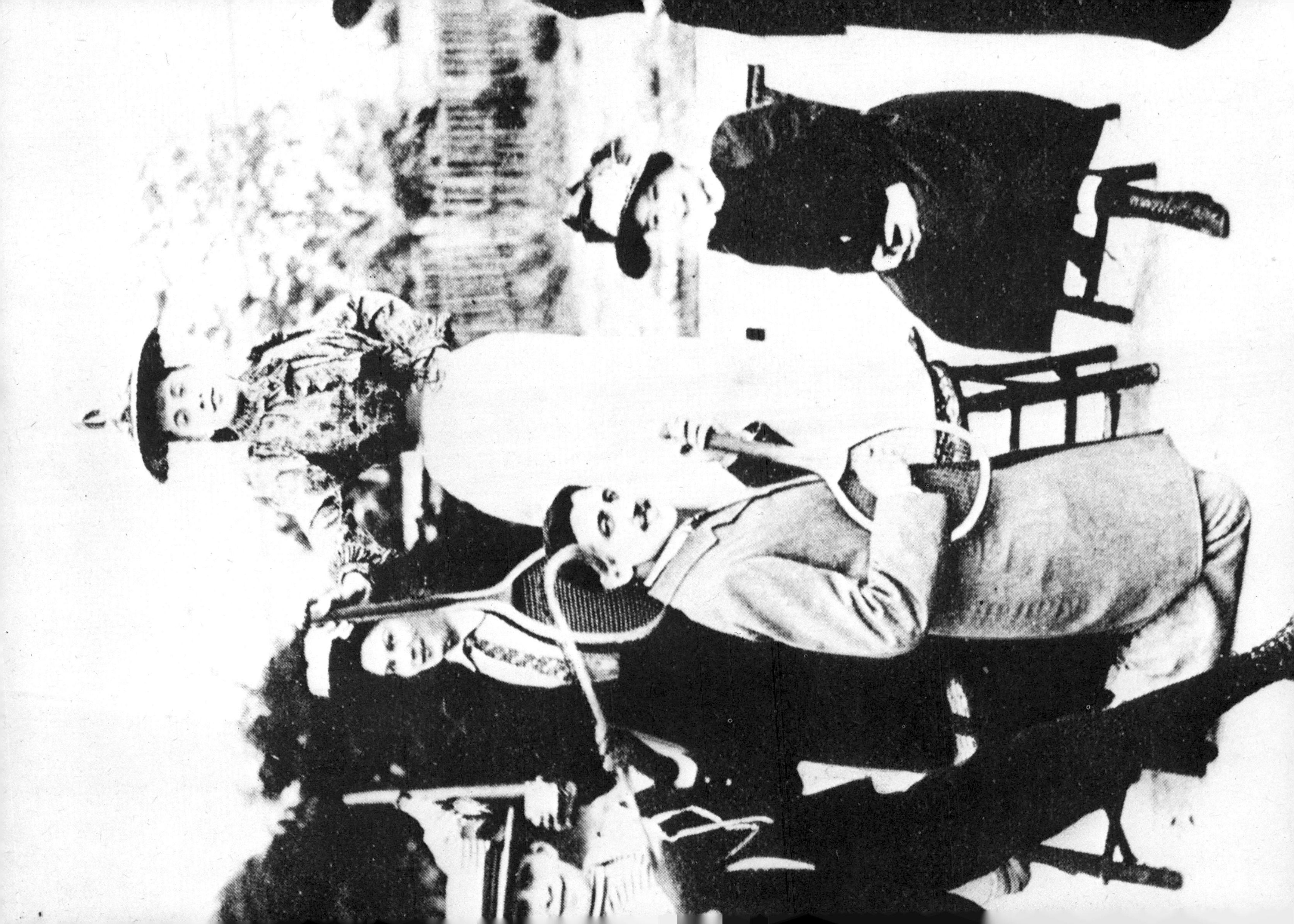

Henri Bergson's lectures in philosophy at the College of Political Science were much more important to A la recherche du temps perdu *in their effect upon the structure of the novel than any other intellectual influence felt by Marcel Proust. They were cousins by marriage and although it would seem he were Bergotte in the book, it is a similarity of the name only, for that philospher's ideas are more closely akin to Ruskin, Bourget and Anatole France.*

'Your very respectful, ardent and captivated Marcel Proust.' He had sensed the desperate need for admiration that consumed Montesquiou and he gratified it generously: 'You are so very much more than the exquisite decadent that people take you for. . . . The one superior person in your world. . . . The greatest art critic for a very long time. . . . Sometimes cornelian, sometimes hermetic. . . . Your soul is a garden of rare, selected blooms. . . .'

He begged a favour in return for such lavish praise: 'Will you be kind enough to introduce me to some of those ladies in whose company you are so often to be seen: the Comtesse Greffuhle, the Princesse de Léon. . . .' The Comtesse Greffuhle, née Caraman-Chimay, had a particular fascination for Marcel. Montesquiou arranged for him to be invited to a party where Marcel glimpsed

Ruskin's influence upon the young Proust was profound, and among other things, the art historian's admiration for Botticelli deeply affected Proust. He often likened the appearance of several of the women in his work to the features found in Botticelli's pictures.

Proust's only visit to Venice occurred in April, 1900. Guided, so often as he was, by Ruskin that he determined, from having read only the previous year, Fors Clavigera, *to see for himself the magnificent Giottos in the Scrovengi Chapel in Padua. Later, in* The Fugitive, *he compared the aerial dog fights during the first World War to those swooping, diving, grief stricken angels in the fresco.*

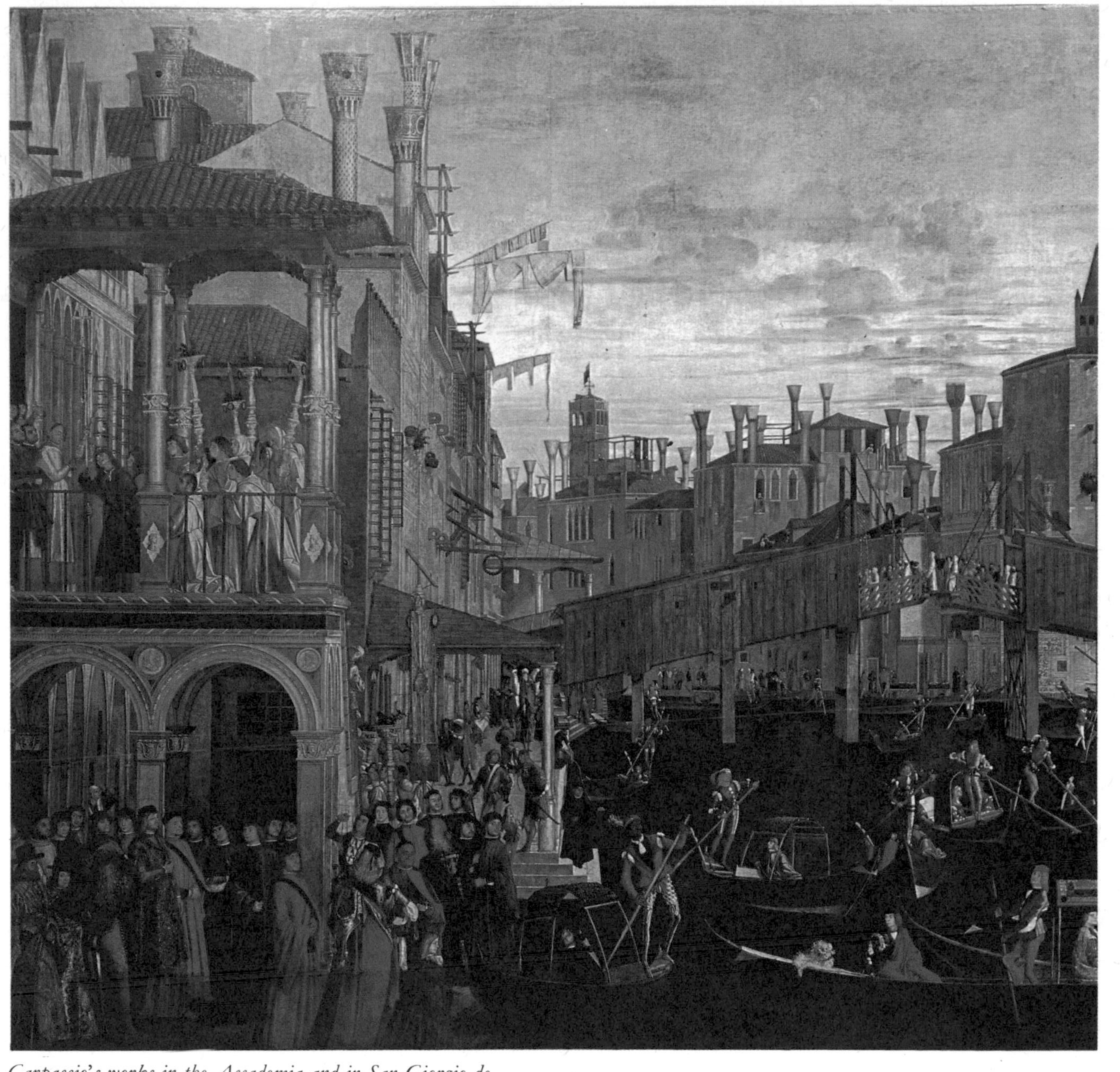

Carpaccio's works in the Accademia and in San Giorgio de Schiavone moved him no less to write long letters home describing them in detail, among them this of the Ceremony of the True Cross.

In 1899 for his own use, Proust laboriously set to work on a translation of the fourth chapter of Ruskin's Bible of Amiens. *Therefore in November 1900 he scrupulously followed his mentor's instruction on making a pilgrimage to what his master termed the French equivalent of the Venetian Gothic. Studying the sculpture of the west front he found a respresentation of the Christ crushing beneath his foot a dragon, and transformed this into the crest of the Baron de Charlus.*

Over the years Proust toured the Norman and Britanny countryside searching out cathedrals. In 1901, driven by his beloved chauffeur Agostinelli it was Lisieux. St Peter's was begun in 1170 and is like Chartres in that one of its noble towers was remodelled in the sixteenth century.

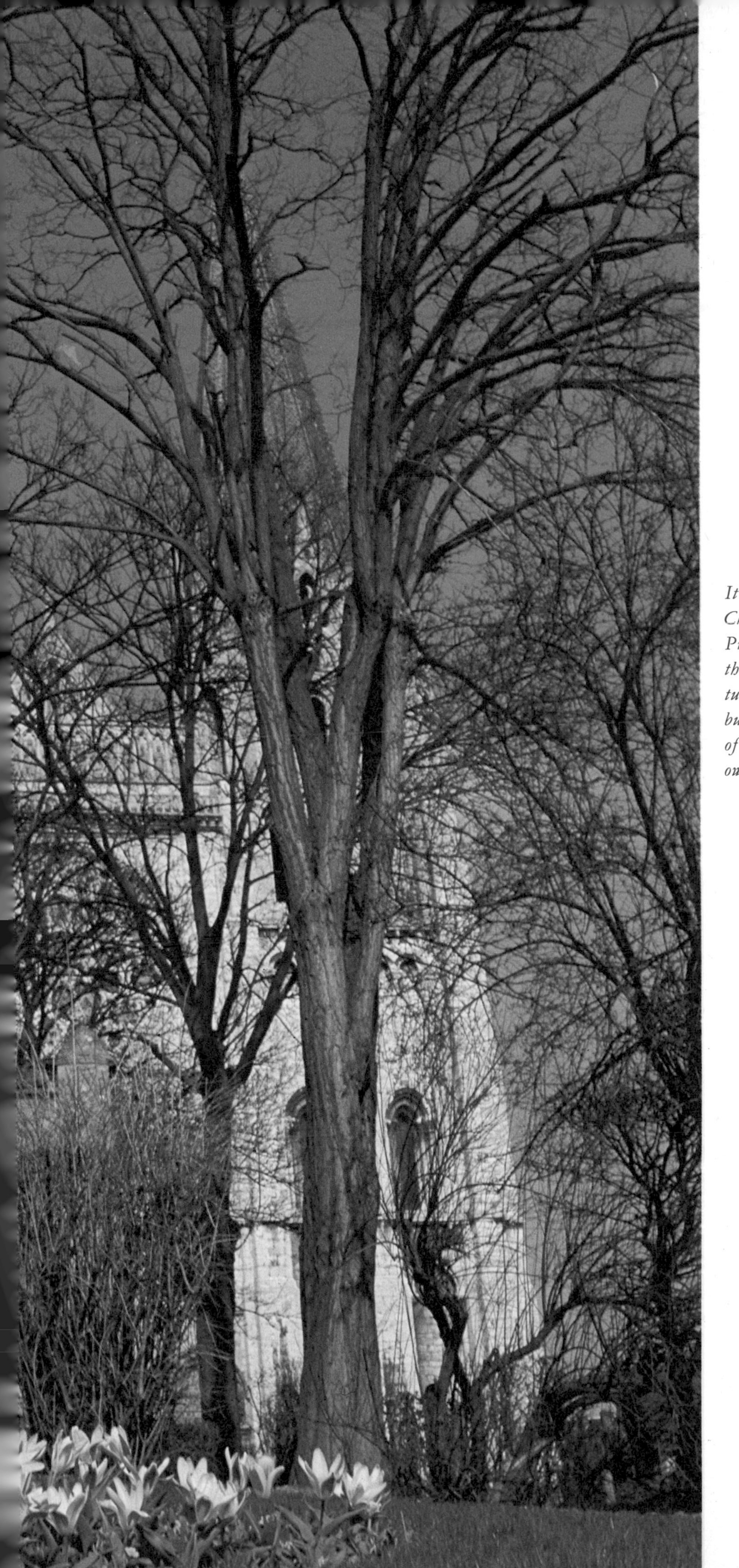

It was in March, 1902, on a visit to Chartres with a group of friends that Proust's awareness of his powers of thought began to take a firmer shape. His tutelage under Ruskin had been beneficial, but now at last he could relate his vision of the present with special reference to his own past.

Proust first met Reynaldo Hahn at Madeleine Lemaire's in 1894. She fostered their relationship that same year when they spent a holiday with her at the Château de Réveillon. The August of the following year the three spent August at her seaside villa in Dieppe. Then, as now, the fashionable promenade on the seafront was just outside the old town gates, while the medieval quarters, cramped and congested huddled around the cathedral within the town's ramparts.

The Abbey of the Magdalen at Vézelay 'solitary on top of a mountain dominating the countryside for miles around in a landscape of incredible harmony, looks more like a Turkish bath than Notre Dame.' wrote Proust in September, 1902, when these photographs were taken. At that time the tympanum from within the west front porch was in the Trocadero Museum in Paris.

in her the future Princesse de Guermantes: 'Her hair was dressed with a Polynesian grace, with purple orchids cascading to the nape of her neck like the "flowered hats" of Monsieur Renan.' 'She is difficult to assess, because to assess means to compare and there is nothing about her that resembles anyone else, *anywhere*. But the whole mystery of her beauty lies in the magnificence and in the enigmatic quality of her eyes. I have never seen such a beautiful woman.' The desire to write was always there. On evenings when he sat 'at the bottom of the table' in houses where he was invited for his wit, 'the Brichots, the Saniettes, the Norpois held forth in front of the shining gilt fenders' of Madame Straus or Madame de Caillavet. At that time the 'stars of the dinner table' were Bourget, France, Brochard, Vogüé, Maupassant, Porto-Riche, Hervieu, Hermant, Vandérem. Marcel Proust worshipped at their shrine and took their measure. On their part, amazed at the depth of his

Earlier, in March, 1902, a party of friends made a sortie to the northeast of Paris to see Laon. The cathedral is famous for the eight oxen in the twin towers, commemorating the beasts that dragged the stones for its construction. The photographs are contemporary.

intelligence, they regretted that he was not working more. 'What did you do, Monsieur France,' Proust asked, 'What did you do to know so much?'

'It's quite simple, my dear Marcel: when I was your age, I wasn't good-looking like you; nobody cared for me; I didn't go out in society and I stayed at home reading all the time.' Marcel did not read all the time, but he was already writing. Several years later he was to gather together under the modest and melancholy title *Les Plaisirs et les Jours*, essays, portraits and stories which he was by now beginning to publish in fashionable literary reviews. It was a charming book, of a slightly old-fashioned elegance and a style that was sometimes too exquisite, but, in it, one was able to detect, locked as in a chrysalis, the great themes of his major work. The volume was expensive, the author little known, the presentation too elaborate. *Les Plaisirs et les Jours* passed unnoticed.

LE PORTRAIT DU JOUR

(Photo H. Manuel.)

REYNALDO HAHN

La maitresse de maison demandait, sur un ton de prière :

— Dites, Reynaldo... *La Tour Saint-Jacques...* ou *La Barchetta ?...*

Alors, après quelque indocilité de chat, il s'asseyait au piano, allumait une cigarette et, tout en la gardant aux lèvres, il chantait.

Aussitôt, du fond du salon, du fumoir, les invités venaient se grouper autour de ce jeune musicien si prodigieusement doué, de cet élève de Massenet qui ajoutait aux grâces de la mélodie à la mode la science du classicisme et l'intelligence de l'art moderne.

— Encore, Reynaldo, encore !...

Et quand il se sentait en confiance, parmi des gens dignes de l'écouter, et capables de le comprendre, quand ses amis, tout proches, créaient autour de lui l'atmosphère de l'intimité, il jouait inlassablement. Il chantait sans fatigue, mêlant les rythmes d'Offenbach aux flonflons des cafés-concerts démodés, imitant Paulus et Darcier, pour passer ensuite à Mozart, à Lulli, à Schumann.

Merveilleuse aisance que la sienne ! Eclatant témoignage des dons les plus heureux ! Quelle joie c'était alors d'entendre la façon dont le piano docile se veloutait sous ses doigts et d'écouter cette voix expressive et chaleureuse, où l'émotion passait, retenue comme par une sorte de pudeur ; où les sons mesurés s'exhalaient avec une autorité câline...

Depuis lors, Reynaldo est devenu Monsieur Reynaldo Hahn, l'auteur de *L'Ile du Rêve*, de *La Carmélite*, de *La Pastorale*, et de tant d'œuvres où s'atteste le parfait développement d'un musicien nourri de science, et pourtant affranchi. On l'appelle maître. Sa célébrité lui a valu des relations commerciales dont il a su tirer profit. *Voici des fruits, des fleurs* fut son « Vase brisé ». Ses *Chansons grises* sont, comme dit l'autre, « sur tous les pianos ». Il est du jury du Conservatoire. Il sera membre de l'Institut.

Pourtant, à le voir, on retrouve en lui l'impérissable jeunesse d'âme, cette jeunesse qui lui donnait tant de séduisante spontanéité lorsque, autrefois, la cigarette aux lèvres, il fredonnait exquisement l'invocation de *La Belle Hélène* ou quelque barcarolle vénitienne, d'une voix souple comme le vol d'une hirondelle rejoignant parfois son reflet sur le miroir de la lagune...

Paul REBOUX.

CHRONIQUE

Centenaire de Gabriel Fauré

par Reynaldo HAHN

UNE unanimité d'admiration s'est formée enfin autour de Fauré ! Plus heureux que ce très grand musicien, — l'un des plus grands, — Debussy et Ravel ont, depuis bien des années, cessé d'être épluchés, discutés, maintenus en observation. Le *Dignus es intrare* leur a été octroyé il y a longtemps déjà et ils étaient consacrés sans conteste alors que Fauré inspirait encore quelque méfiance à ceux qui traitent de vieilles niaiseries le souci de la forme, la richesse du vocabulaire, l'élégance et la pureté du style.

Par bonheur, la plupart des compositeurs qui représentent actuellement le « modernisme » le plus impérieux se sont ralliés à Fauré. A vrai dire, on ne sait trop comment cela s'est fait... Mais qu'importe ! Il convient de s'en réjouir puisque leur suffrage a entraîné celui de leurs partisans. Et puis, pourquoi le fauréisme n'aurait-il pas, tout comme le gaullisme, ses adhérents imprévus ?

Quoi qu'il en soit, nous nous préparons, dans une entente générale, à fêter le centenaire du merveilleux poète et de l'homme adorable que fut Gabriel Fauré ; et voici que le triomphe de la paix et le retour du printemps illuminent d'un rayonnement suprême cette enthousiaste glorification.

Pendant toute une semaine, du 11 au 17 de ce mois, des manifestations d'une haute qualité artistique se succéderont en l'honneur du maître qui nous est si cher. Sous l'ardente et puissante impulsion de Mme Marguerite Long, le Comité d'action du Centenaire, qui remplace en quelque sorte la Société des Amis de Fauré, fondée naguère par Mme Henry de Jouvenel, a élaboré un programme digne de la grande mémoire qu'on se propose de célébrer (1).

Quelle joie de pouvoir communier en Fauré d'une âme apaisée, d'écouter sa voix profonde et douce d'une oreille où s'est tu l'imaginaire écho des canonnades meurtrières !

En vérité, on a peine à se figurer ce qu'il aurait pu ressentir s'il eût vécu les années d'horreur qui viennent de s'écouler. L'idée seule d'un rapprochement quelconque entre sa personne et cette époque abominable révolte le cœur. Je crois, pour ma part, qu'il n'aurait même pas compris ce qui se passait ! Rien, certes, de la tristesse, de la douleur ne lui était inconnu, — il l'a prouvé dans bien des pages poignantes, et il avait, comme il l'a montré aussi, le sens du tragique. Mais les tristesses, les douleurs mornes et sordides auxquelles l'humanité a été soumise et le tragique abject de cette guerre, il n'eût pu les concevoir, ou bien il n'y aurait pas survécu.

J'ai eu bien souvent déjà l'occasion d'écrire sur Fauré et j'espère bien le faire encore à loisir, ici, dans ce journal où il écrivit lui-même pendant si longtemps, exerçant son métier de critique avec une clairvoyance et une équité infaillibles, mais aussi avec une indulgence, à peine ironique parfois, un tact et une modestie qui devraient servir d'exemple aujourd'hui à certains musiciens quand ils émettent des jugements et surtout quand ils parlent d'eux-mêmes. Il aurait bien ri — j'entends encore son rire un peu enroué de fumeur obstiné ! — s'il avait vu des apprentis promus au rang de maîtres et si on lui avait appris qu'un jeune compositeur, au début de sa carrière, se croyait autorisé, quels que pussent être ses mérites, à publier un ouvrage en deux volumes intitulé « Technique de *mon langage musical* »... J'ai beaucoup connu Fauré, je l'ai beaucoup fréquenté et je ne lui ai jamais entendu parler de *son* langage musical. En existe-t-il pourtant de plus original, de plus naturellement ingénieux, de plus beau et de plus singulier ? En connaît-on un seul pourtant qui soit plus digne d'une étude sagace et minutieuse ? Il est à souhaiter qu'on la fasse un jour. Mais c'est une tâche qui exige des aptitudes exceptionnelles et celui qui l'entreprendrait ne manquerait pas d'éprouver, au moment d'expliquer par des mots les mystères du style fauréen, le tremblement qui saisissait Léonard quand il prenait ses pinceaux...

Reynaldo HAHN, *de l'Institut.*

(1) Voir au Courrier des Spectacles le programme de ces manifestations.

From their first meeting in the summer of 1894 Reynaldo Hahn and Proust were attracted to each other. The young Venezuelan composer-pianist-singer was very popular in the fashionable salons of the Faubourg, and frequently accompanied himself when singing his own compositions, as well as playing trios. The relationship between the writer and musician began with fervour and in the first years they were seldom apart or without being in contact with each other by telephone or letter. Hahn's niece, the Comtesse de Forceville, lives in his flat kept, as a memorial, exactly as it had been when he inhabited it.

Friendships

From 1892 to 1900, Proust's way of life was modified slowly and surely, by illness. His attacks of asthma increased in number and intensity. There were still, however, long periods of respite between them that allowed him to lead an almost normal life, to go out in society, to stay with his great-uncle at Auteuil, with Madame Straus or the banker, Hugo Finaly, at Trouville, or to go to Evian. He even made trips into the French countryside, and later to Holland and Italy. As the attacks, however, were more violent by day than by night, and particularly in the summer, they forced him, little by little, to adopt hours of working and of entertaining his friends, that were like no-one else's. He lived with his parents, at 9, boulevard Malesherbes:

'. . . a large solid house, whose apartments had that comfortable roominess characteristic of the houses of the prosperous bourgeoisie in the years 1890–1900. The impression I have kept of it, and which I see the moment I close my eyes, is of a rather dark interior, crammed with heavy furniture, smothered in curtains and muffled by carpets, and all in black and red—in fact, it was an apartment not so very far removed as we think it was from the dark bric-à-brac of Balzac. . . .'

Although Doctor Proust's face was coarser now with age—it was framed by a grey beard and sported a moustache that was still black—it had retained the nobility of one of Holbein's merchant princes. His second son, Robert, looked very like him and was making good progress with his studies in surgery. Between Marcel and his mother there was an unbreakable bond; he lived like a child in a state of utter dependence on her. Their embraces and emotional displays frequently had an impatient and unhappy witness in Doctor Proust. To appease 'Papa' had always been one of the first concerns of mother and son. Theirs was a sweet, continuing complicity. When Marcel could not sleep, he would write letters to her and leave them in the hall for her to find in the morning; then and only then could he rest. Gradually, his circle of friends was widening, little by little he was making progress both in the world of letters and in high society. Those were the days of 'that simple and lovely renaissance, à la Massenet and Dumas fils' that went from Sarcey and Gounod, to Daudet and Maupassant, then to Bourget and Loti. Proust, who had always loved Alphonse Daudet as France's Dickens, met him at the house of Madame Arthur Baignères; henceforth he and Reynaldo Hahn became regular visitors at the 'Thursdays' in the rue de Bellechasse. The writer's sons liked him very much, particularly Lucien the younger of the two. They had the same sharp sense of humour, the same horror of those vulgar phrases that 'set the teeth on edge and make one squint', and which they both called 'squinters': '*La grande bleue* or *La Côte d'Azur* for the Mediterrancan, *Albion* for England, *The Emerald Isle* for Ireland, *nos petits soldats* for the French army, *le rocher de Guernesey* for exile, and all the words of *La Paimpolaise*, etc.' It was also a 'squinter' for anyone who knew no English to take his leave with a casual '*Bye-Bye*'. 'Squinters' sent the two friends into gales of laughter, which Marcel would attempt to hide behind his glove, but which in front of vulnerable people, became embarrassing. One one occasion, they had to make their getaway, doubled up with laughter, under the stern, suspicious eye of Montesquiou who never forgave them. Lucien Daudet was well aware of his friend's peculiarities, his detailed, if somewhat wild and woolly ideas on sartorial elegance. ('Be careful how you dress,' Madame Adrien Proust wrote to him 'and above all, no more wearing your hair like a Frankish King.') He was however quick to counter the accusations of those people who hardly knew Proust at all but described him as *for ever* ravenous for gossip, *for ever* dressed in some outlandish fashion with pieces of cotton wool sticking out of his collar, which he kept turned up for fear of the cold, *for ever* guilty of fantastic compliments and of distributing ridiculous tips. It was perfectly true that sometimes a scrap of cotton wool might find its way out of his collar and that his friends would smile and push it down again with a reproachful 'Marcel!' It was true that one evening he borrowed a hundred francs from the

hall porter at the Ritz and then whispered: 'Keep it, it was for you.' But those who were fond of him paid no attention to these harmless eccentricities. They admired in him 'an almost child-like sensitiveness, delightful simplicity, a natural distinction that could not be disguised, a nobility of heart', a habit of politeness that embraced the humble and the mighty alike (he addressed a letter, for example, to 'Monsieur le Concierge de Monsieur le Duc de Guiche'); a generosity which involved him spending hours, when he was giving a present, choosing the very prettiest, the most suitable gift which had to come from the very best shop: 'Flowers or fruit for a woman had to come from Lemaître or from Charton, compôtes for a sick friend from Tanrade. A handkerchief he had borrowed

Niece of Napoleon, daughter of Jerome, the Princesse Mathilde was notable for her ancestry, her salon, her meddlesomeness in politics and her almost public affaires. *Her complaisant husband was the immensely rich Russian, Count Demidoff, an art connoisseur of the first rank whose collection, housed outside Florence, is one of the finest in the world. She said of herself that if it had not been for her uncle she'd have been selling oranges in the streets of Ajaccio.*

had a very suspicious nature, and there had developed in him a certain contempt for humanity which work and comparative solitude were to magnify out of all proportion, and which prevented him on many occasions from discriminating between those who were capable of meanness and those who were not. . . .' Once he had given his trust, however, an almost child-like gaiety and the deep nobility of his character were very touching. The close friends that Lucien Daudet met most frequently at the boulevard Malesherbes were Reynaldo Hahn, Robert de Billy, the painter Frédéric de Madrazo ('Coco Madrazo') and Robert de Flers. The two brothers, Marcel and Robert, were excellent friends. Although in day to day family squabbles Robert always sided with his father, while the mother took Marcel's part 'the affection they had for one another brought home to us the meaning of the term *brotherly love.*'

In 1895, to please Professor Proust, who had longed for so many years to see him choose a profession, Marcel agreed to sit for a comprehensive examination for the post of 'unpaid attaché' at the

Bibliothèque Marzarine. He proved to be the most detached of attachés and took one leave of absence after another. Lucien Daudet would often go and collect him at the Institute and they would go together to the Louvre or to a classical matinée at the Comédie-Française. Marcel would be carrying a vaporiser full of some antiseptic or other, and would hold forth in front of the pictures, pointing out to Lucien Daudet the beauty of Fra Angelico's colours, which he described as 'creamy and comestible' or the difference between Rembrandt's two *Philosophers.* He was an excellent art critic, although no one knew it at the time. What he saw in a canvas, both pictorially and intellectually, was always beautiful and communicable. It was not an arbitrary, personal impression, it was the unforgettable, the very essence of the picture. . . .' 'And then he would suddenly stop in front of the gentleman with the red nose and the red gown who smiled at a child and he would exclaim 'But it's the living image of Monsieur du Lau! What an incredible likeness! Wouldn't it be nice if it were really he! Ah, my friend,' he would go on, with that twitch he had of the nostrils and the high spirits of a young animal that he sometimes displayed, as if somewhere in him he had untapped reserves of the sporting open-air life, 'What fun it is to look at pictures!'

The great sorrow of this period was the death of his grandmother. Proust and his mother had been united in their admiration for this remarkable woman, more Sévigné than Sévigné herself. *Madame Adrien Proust to Marcel*: 'Sometimes I come across words or passages in Madame de Sévigné which give me particular pleasure. She says (in criticism of a friend, and the friend's relationship with her son). "I know another mother who never thought of herself and who lived entirely for her children." Don't you think that applies to your grandmother? Only she would never have said it. . . .' The death of her mother produced, in Madame Proust, a sudden, touching transformation. 'It is not enough to say that all her gaiety had gone; she seemed to melt into the shape of some sort of imploring image and to be afraid to raise her voice in case she offended the mournful presence that never left her side. . . .' Suddenly she began to resemble the departed, possibly

The physical characteristics, the wide thin mouth, the bird quality of the long thin neck and nose, the blond hair, the elegance, the remoteness combined with wit of the Comtesse Laure de Chevigné (here seen with her hand on her hip) are the principle embodiments of the more exalted Duchesse de Guermantes.

If the elegance of Comtesse de Greffulhe and her stunning good looks were the inspiration for the portrait of the Princesse de Guermantes, it was her position at the apex of Parisian society—friend of Edward VII—and her relationship to Count Robert de Montesquiou, that more accurately explain the social status of the Duchesse de Guermantes.

because her great grief had hastened a natural change in her features and the appearance of someone she already carried in her, or because sorrow suggested to her features traits which had always potentially been there. With her mother dead, she would not have wished to be other than the person she had so admired. She went to Cabourg and read the *Letters* of Madame de Sévigné, sitting on the beach where her mother had sat and reading from the volume her mother had carried everywhere. Shrouded in crêpe, she proceeded 'all in black, with timid, pious steps, along the sands the beloved feet had trodden before her and she had the air of searching for someone the waves were going to return to her. . . .' Although her mourning was strict, however, she did not expect the same of her family. It was enough that they were true to their own feelings.

How did he spend his time? First and foremost he wrote letters 'mad, magic letters', letters that were commanding, wheedling, 'questioning, breathless', ingenious and witty, letters which flat-

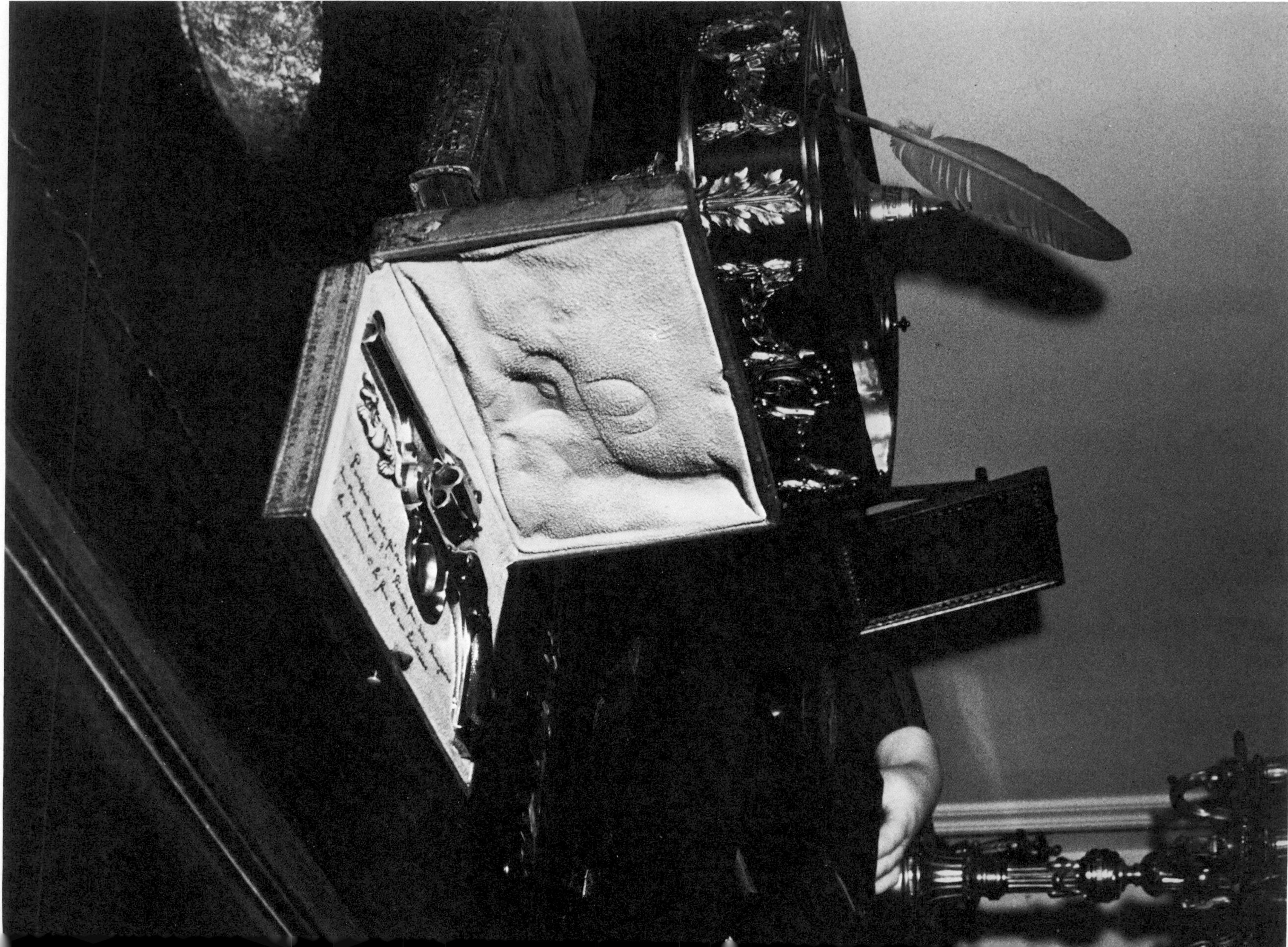

When Armand de Gramont, as Duc de Guiche, was to marry Elaine, daughter of the Comtesse de Greffulhe he asked for a wedding present 'The only thing I don't have—a revolver.' The pistol was made by the best gunsmith in Paris, Gastinne-Renette, and boxed in a case painted by Coco de Madrazo. His son Antoine, the present Duc de Gramont, and his son Antoine the present Duc de Guiche are in front of the Laszlo portrait of Armand.

Robert de Rothschild became a literary friend of Proust when the latter was at the height of his fame. One of his sons married the granddaughter of Proust's friend Madame Léon Fould, who was famous for her collection of glass and porcelain as well as the charm of her salon. Her portrait, by Renoir, is to be found in her grandson Baron Max Fould-Springer's home, here seen with his sister Baronne Elie de Rothschild.

Like her grandmother the Comtesse de Chevigné and several other of her ancestresses the Vicomtesse de Noailles is named Laure after the Marquise Laure de Sade. Here she is dressed as a Muse receiving her guests at a costume ball. She and her husband were ardent supporters of the surrealist movement, he in fact produced one of Buñuel's early films, L'Age d'or.
Her daughter, also named Laure, is the Comtesse de la Haye Jousselin, here with her elder son Edmond, who maintains the family interest in the arts.

tered the vanity of the recipient, disturbed him by the irony of his flights of fancy, tormented him by their lack of trust and charmed him by their style. The charm must have overcome the disquiet, for people were keeping those letters twenty years before he became famous, and after he died, these buried treasures began to emerge from cupboards all over Paris. His letters were frequently reproachful. 'Marcel Proust's the Devil himself,' Alphonse Daudet said one day, referring to his uncanny and disturbing facility for analysing people's motives. He was a trying friend: 'Sometimes one wounded him without meaning to,' said Lauris. 'The trouble was, he had no confidence in other people. He was always imagining you were holding something back, that you were cold towards him. Heaven only knows what he suspected!' The reproaches

1899. At the back are Prince Edmond de Polignac, Princesse de Brancovan, Marcel Proust, Prince Constantin de Brancovan, Léon Delafosse; seated are Mme de Montgemord, Princesse de Polignac, Comtesse Mathieu de Noailles; on the ground are Princesse de Caraman Chimay and Abel Hermant. Part of the characteristics of Bergotte derive from Edmond de Polignac, whose wife was the sewing machine heiress, Winaretta Singer, and a great deal of Delafosse went into the making of the musician Morel

arrived by letter. A friend might leave him at two o'clock in the morning and would wake up to find a fat envelope, brought by his concierge, lying on the breakfast tray and a letter analysing, with a pitiless clarity, all that had been said and left unsaid. His invalid's life, his 'interminable sleepless nights' encouraged the work of his imagination on the motives that prompted his own actions and those of his family and friends, and engendered in him that *genius for suspicion*, described by all who knew him well. In the outside world, he continued to play his rôle of 'genealogist and entymologist' of French Society. New faces were being added to the original circle of friends. The young Duc de Guiche, a man who represented the best of the eighteenth century, and was more interested in optics and hydrostatics than in social tittle-tattle, had known him

FONDATION SINGER-POLIGNAC
CREEE LE 25 MARS 1928
PAR LA PRINCESSE EDMOND DE POLIGNAC
NEE WINNARETTA SINGER
1865 - 1943

L'Original qui aime bien le petit Marcel Louisa

Avril 1904

Louisa de Mornand is to be found in Rachel the magnificent actress who drove St Loup mad with love and also one of the many facets of Albertine. In life she was the mistress of the Marquis Louis d'Albuféra (also an original of St Loup) and for eighteen months she had an affaire *with Proust.*

as 'the obscure young man who sat at the bottom of Madame Straus' table.' Another object of his fulsomeness was the Comtesse de Noailles, a fine poet and a brilliant and vivacious beauty with a bold, biting wit, who was won over at once by 'his magnificent intelligence, his tenderness, his superlative gifts'. Who knew better than he how to find her latest collection of poems superior to the one before and to justify the increased enthusiasm by the most subtle of arguments? And who understood better than he that the poet was the woman herself? About the same time, he met Antoine Bibesco, a Rumanian prince whom Marcel thought was 'the most intelligent of Frenchmen', and his brother, Emmanuel Bibesco. There were intimate, jealous friendships with something of the secret society in their nature. They had a vocabulary all of their own. In their language the Bibescos were the Oscebib; Marcel, Lecram; Bertrand de Fénelon, Nolenef. A secret was 'a tomb' and to 'play the hyena' was to 'violate a tomb'. To introduce a newcomer to the circle was 'to effect a conjunction'. Later, the Bibescos 'effected a conjunction' between their cousin Marthe, a young woman as beautiful as she was talented, and Marcel. It was she who made the observation that for Marcel, who was so much the prisoner of ill-health, the Bibescos and Reynaldo Hahn were the purveyors of dreams and his mirror up to life.

It is symbolic that he was still living in the room he'd had as a child and he worked, as he had always done, on the dining room table. His father was a very busy man and left the house early in the morning so Marcel could stay in bed without fear of his mother 'turning him out' of it. It was only after breakfast that he managed to dress and to button his boots, which for him, an asthmatic, was a particularly difficult operation. In the evening, if he were unwell and not going out, he was to be found in the dining room, sitting at the table with its red cover, beside a roaring fire, and writing in a school exercise-book beneath a Carcel lamp that

Anna de Noailles' bust by Rodin and a photograph taken five years after Proust and she first met. He was an ardent and effusive admirer of her poetry and valued her friendship doubly because of that and her social connections. Descended from an ancient aristocratic Greek family, she was the daughter of Grégroire de Brancovan and allied several times over to Montesquiou and the Bibesco family.

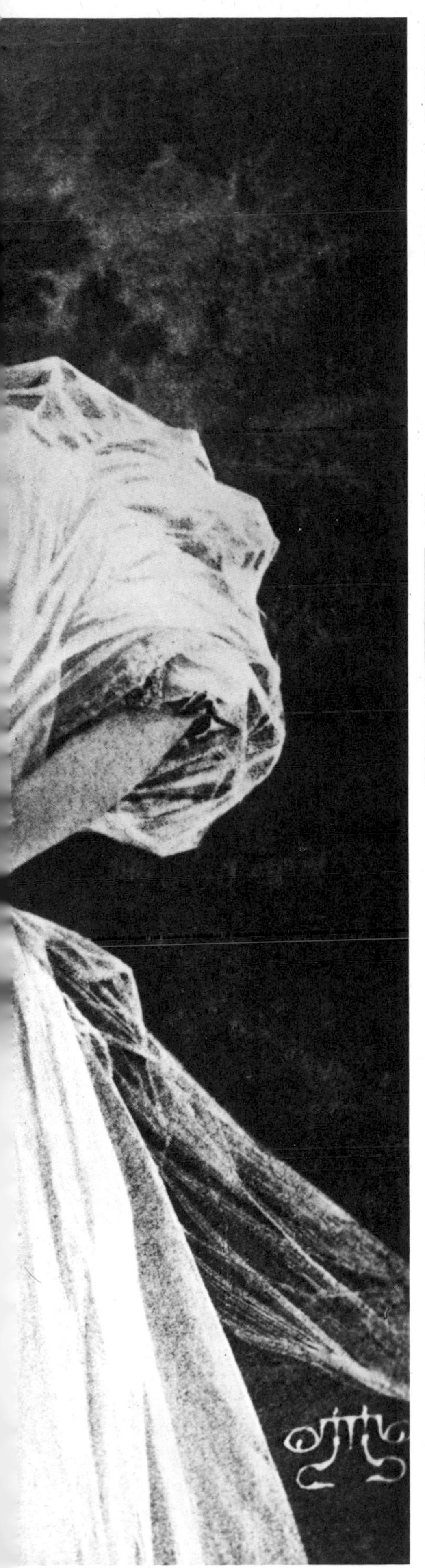

The Princesse Eugénie de Brancovan who bears a remarkable resemblance to her aunt Anna de Noailles, like all the Brancovans lives in the Ile St Louis, is here photographed as she leaves the home of friends, other 'Proustians', the Ruspolis.

he loved for its soft light. Beside him, Madame Proust would be half asleep in an armchair. There was an element of infantilism in this way of life, but to remain a child is to become a poet. When he was well enough, he dined out. He was invited out often because he was witty and his imitations were the delight of the salons. 'He used to imitate Montesquiou's laugh and was a great admirer of Madame Greffulhe's which, like the bells of Bruges, flung its peals up into the air in a most unexpected fashion. He used to mimic Madeleine Lemaire seeing her guests to the door: "Madame de Maupeou, you sang like an angel tonight! That Brandès woman is quite astonishing she never looks a day over twenty . . . the little creature is so *artissstic* (speaking of Madrazo) . . . Au revoir, Montesquiou, dear, great poet of poets . . . Atishoo! Be careful, don't catch cold!. . ." Then she would say: "Come along Suzette!" And as she went back up the stairs she would tell her dogs what she really thought of them all.' What Marcel liked best, however, was to give rather solemn dinner parties at his parents' home when, 'around the azaleas and the white lilac' he would gather together the prototypes of Saint-Loup, Bloch and Oriane and such friends as Bourget, Hervieu, Madame de Noailles, Anatole France, Calmette —'and Marcel, in evening dress, his shirt front rumpled, his hair slightly dishevelled, breathing with difficulty, his fine eyes shining but with great shadows round them from his sleeplessness, going out of his way, with the manners of a charming child, to create a happy atmosphere between his ill-assorted guests who did not know one another yet, and beneath their condescension and their flattery, were keeping a wary eye on one another. . . . Often, in the course of the meal, if he were worried (or curious) as to the effect his guests were having on one another, he would move his place from one to the other; he would take his soup beside one of them, and the fish (or a portion of it) by another, and so on until the end of the meal. By the time they came to the fruit, one imagines he had been round them all. It was a token of his courtesy, of goodwill towards them all, for he would have been miserable if anyone had had cause to complain; and he wished to pay each one a special compliment and to assure himself, with his usual perspicacity, that

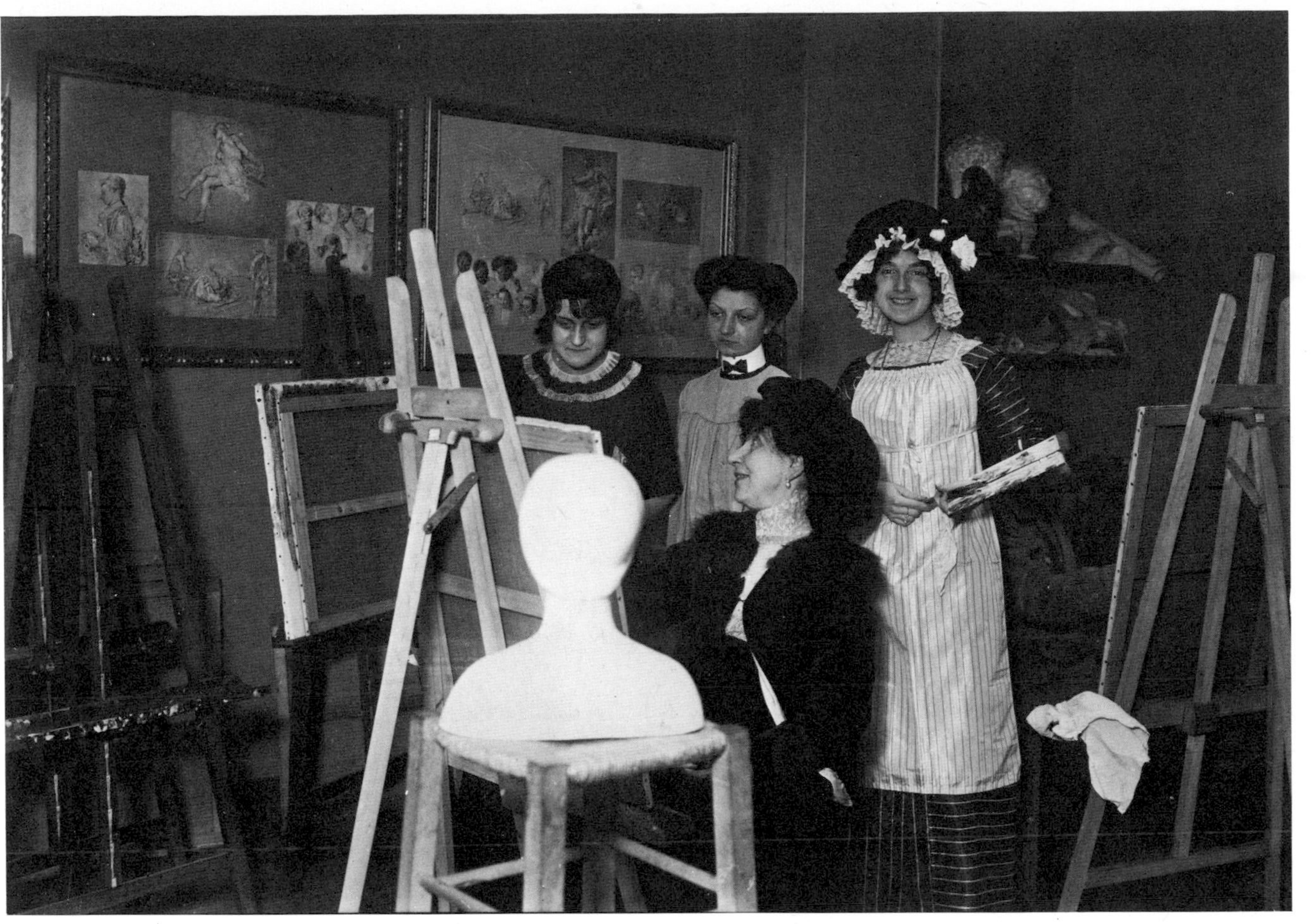

It was said of Madeleine Lemaire (seated at the easel) that she painted more roses than God created. Protectress of artists, she was a firm friend of Reynaldo and Proust. The somewhat 'artistic' décor of her homes and her passionate dedication to the role of hostess and dread of 'bores' are to be found in Mme de Villeparisis and especially in Mme Verdurin.

each person's particular aura was favourable to the well-being of the whole. The results, moreover, were excellent and one was never bored at his house. . . .'

Quarrels

That was Marcel Proust around 1898. The umbilical cord was still unbroken and he continued to need, for life itself, the emotional nourishment provided daily by his mother's love. But, although his life at home was that of a child, he was perfectly capable of behaving in the most virile fashion on occasions that demanded courage. 'I took after my grandmother,' says the Narrator who here is identified with the author, 'in that I was devoid of personal pride to such a degree that I might easily have been thought devoid of dignity. But I learned in the end, through life's experience, that it was a mistake to smile sweetly when someone mocked me and not to be resentful. Anger and malice were quite another matter and came to me in sudden bursts of fury. . . .' Observing how his most worthy friends would deal with those who slighted them he came to show, by his words and his actions, that there was another side to his character, and it was very proud.

A wrong gesture, even a look in a restaurant was enough to make his hackles rise and more than once, such occasions led to a duel. 'I remember the silence round our table, one night at Larue's when he sat there, perfectly calm, his white hand resting without a tremor on the tablecloth, and with the most calculated, most carefully spelt-out insolence in the world, withered a man who he suspected of speaking ill of him and who had come over to shake hands.' In 1897, insulted by Jean Lorrain in a periodical on the subject of his *Plaisirs et les Jours*, he despatched two friends forthwith: the painter, Jean Béraud and Gustave de Borda (nicknamed 'Sword-Thrust Borda'), a marvellous duellist with a charming, flowery wit, and also an incomparable second. The duel was fought with pistols and was inconclusive, but Béraud kept a very clear picture of that wet winter's morning at the Tour de Villebon, and of Proust's crazy pluck in spite of his physical debility. The Dreyfus Affair provided him with further opportunities to show his courage. It sent a wave of anti-semitism throughout France. Proust

Chez la Princesse Mathilde.
Napoleon's niece counted among her admirers so many of the great writers of the middle years of the 1800s that she was nicknamed 'Notre Dame des Arts'. Short and plump, wearing her famous black pearl necklace she had a habit of enthroning herself in the armchair to receive her guests. She was gruff and kind, a stickler for etiquette which she frequently ignored, amorous and vengeful, nevertheless

a good friend and blessed with a sense of humour. When invited to accompany the visiting Tsar Nicholas II to inspect her uncle's tomb she refused, saying 'Thank you very much. I have my own keys.' She appears in A la Recherche du temps perdu *in her own name, and is also partly the Princesse de Parme. Her ineffably stupid lady-in-waiting appears as Mme de Varabon.*

The supreme actress, Berma, was of course the 'divine' Bernhardt.

Reynaldo at the piano.

When about to write in the famous Gramont visiting book, the duc admonished Proust 'Your name only, monsieur, no noble sentiments, please'.

Dandy, aesthete, poet, arbiter of taste, egregious genealogist, snob: *Comte Robert de Montesquiou-Fezenzac—Proust's Baron de Charlus.*

loved his mother too much (and, in any case, was too fair-minded) not to react against it, even if it meant crossing swords with a man whose anger he dreaded, like Robert de Montesquiou. *Proust to Montesquiou*: 'I did not reply yesterday to your question about the Jews. For one very simple reason: although I am a Catholic, like my father and my brother, my mother on the other hand, is a Jewess. You will understand, therefore, that I have every reason for wishing to abstain from discussions of that kind. . . .' On the question of tolerance, he was in perfect agreement with his friend, Madame Straus, who had been brought up 'in the tradition of the Halévy family where all religions had met and been friends for many years.' She herself was not a convert. 'I have too little religion in me,' she said 'to start changing it,' but she had a great respect for other people's beliefs. When the Affair demanded a choice, however, Madame Straus took a firm stand and, in spite of her liking for certain of the 'leading lights of the other side' (Jules Lemaître, Maurice Barrès) she did not attempt to retain in her 'salon' the fanatics who were estranged by her Dreyfus sympathies. On the subject of the Affair, however, his staunchest ally was his mother, who strongly shared his feelings and his faith. Mother and son observed the attitude of friends and of any strangers they met, and attempted, like Bloch in the novel, to guess at the real opinions that lay beneath the surface. In 1899 at Evian, finding himself at the Splendid Hôtel at the same time as the Comte and Comtesse Eu, Proust treated them in the spirit he felt the Affair demanded, but he described them as a novelist. *Proust to Madame Proust*: 'The Eus seem to be very simple, good people though I do not give an inch and keep my hat firmly on my head in their presence.' 'Relations severed since Rennes.' 'Finding myself with the old man in front of a door which one of us had to go through first, I stood aside. And he passed me but raised his hat with a great flourish, neither condescendingly nor in the manner of Haussonville, but simply as

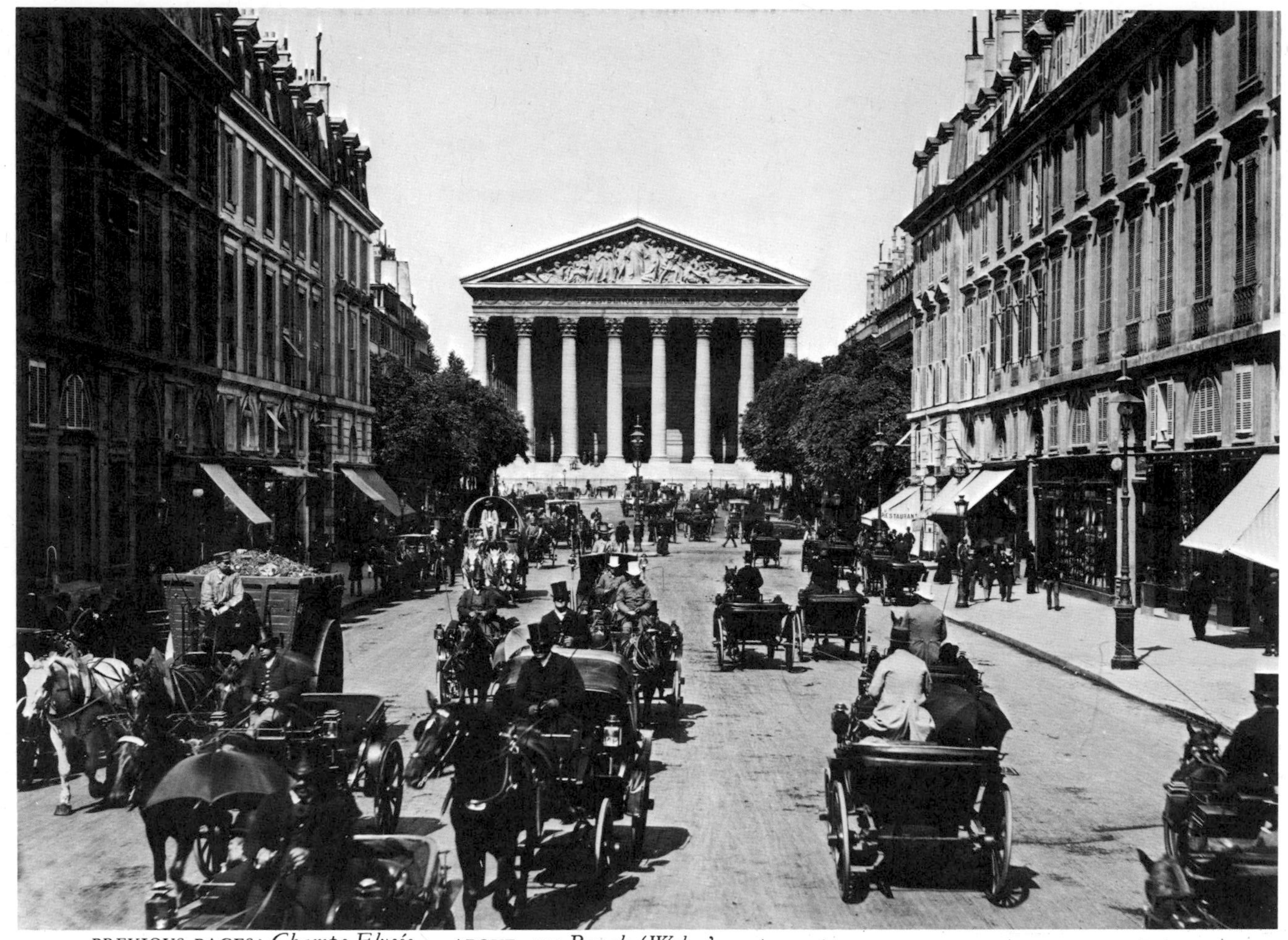

PREVIOUS PAGES: *Champs-Elysée, Rond Point, 1885: Place des Médicis, 1890:* ABOVE, *rue Royale (Weber's restaurant on the left), 1889.*

a decent and very polite old man, a greeting, I may say, as I have never had from other people for whom I have stood aside, and who sweep by, their noses in the air, simple bourgeois though they be.' Although so many Dreyfus sympathisers allowed the Affair to colour all their judgements and became incapable of fairness, even of compassion, towards their adversaries, Marcel Proust retained his sense of proportion. He did not break relations with the Daudet family. When the time came, in 1901, for the reinstatements, he was happy to see that, for Dreyfus and Picquart, life 'had turned out all right in the end, after the fashion of fairy-tales and novelettes', but it distressed him greatly to see Général Mercier insulted by Barthou, 'a Dreyfusard of a few weeks' standing'. And although during the Affair he had come across active hostility, not from the Church but

Boulevard des Italiens at the time of the Great Exposition of 1900.

from certain congregations, he took up the cudgels in *Le Figaro* on behalf of the churches with whom the Briand project was threatening to interfere.

In 1900, Doctor and Madame Adrien Proust moved to a house 'with an echo and a wide staircase' at 45, rue de Courcelles, on the corner of the rue de Monceau. The rooms were vast and sumptuous. In the evening, Marcel worked in the great dining room, panelled in dark mahogany. On the table were books and papers and an oil lamp 'which he loved for its soft, blond light'. He had recently discovered a 19th century English writer, John Ruskin, who was almost unknown in France and whose theories on art delighted him for they coincided with and confirmed his own on many points while, on others, they aroused his critical curiosity. He had decided

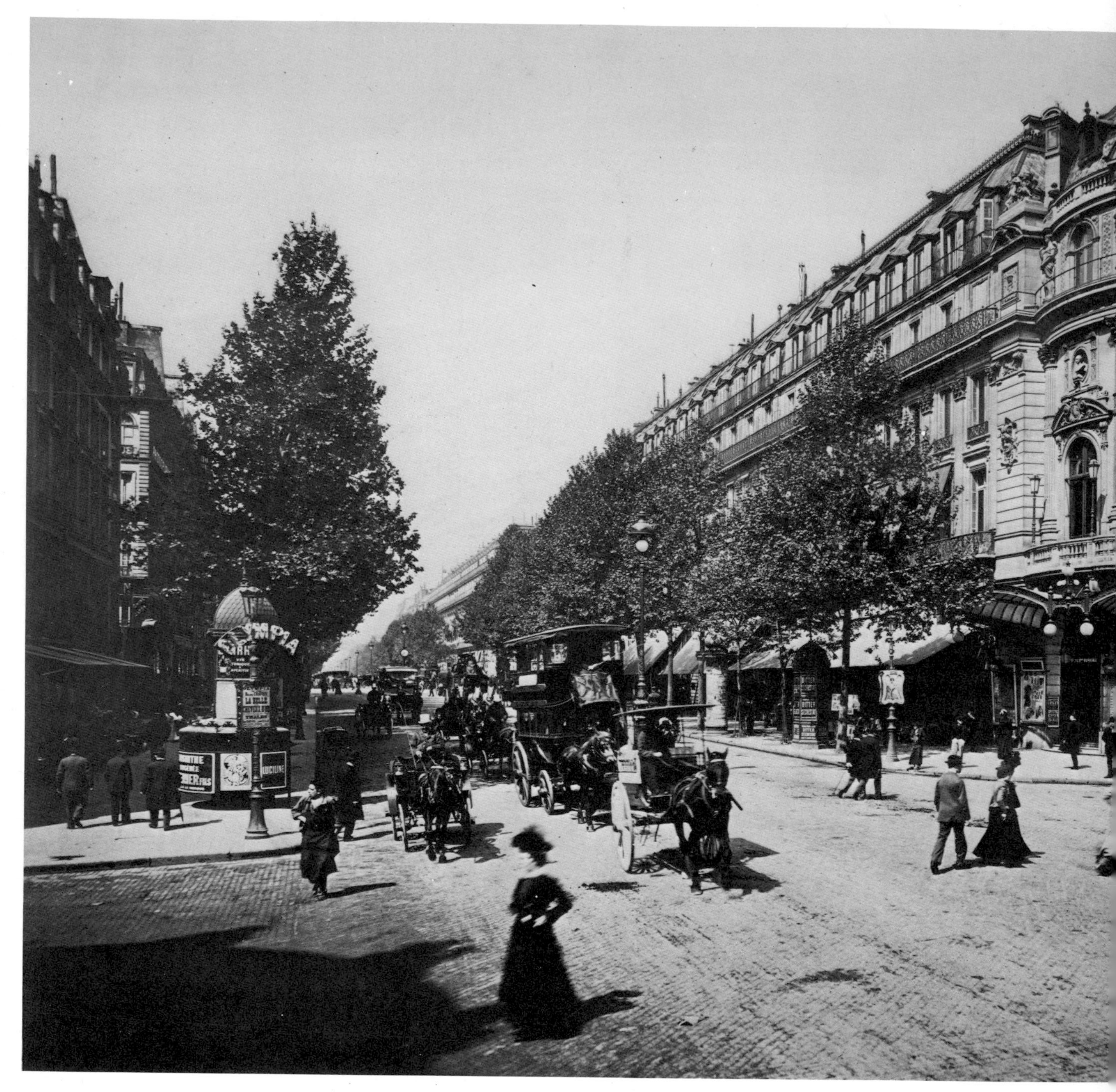

to translate him. There, too, with the electric lights extinguished and the house fast asleep, he read Saint-Simon, Chateaubriand, Saint-Beuve, Emile Mâle. The door was always open to his close friends: Antoine Bibesco, Guiche, Georges de Lauris, Louis d'Albuféra and Bertrand de Fénelon whose bright eyes and flying coat-tails were to become part of the attraction of Saint-Loup.

For a while the Vaudeville theatre in the boulevard des Italiens was Réjane's own. Mistress of comedy, as the 'divine' Sarah was of tragedy, she is one of the composites of Berma. When he was homeless for a while, Proust lived in her house for four months in 1919.

Pretty Louisa de Mornand would come in sometimes, after the theatre, to say goodnight to Marcel. It is remarkable that all of them—actress, diplomat, scholar, poet, and horseman—considered it a privilege to be the friend of this unknown invalid who seemed, through them, to be exploring the world. 'He seemed like a distinguished foreigner surrounded by all the mystery of a land of memory and of thought.' Sometimes Doctor Proust would drop in and tell some political or medical story; Madame Proust, always gentle and shy, would say a pleasant word or two to her son's friends and then withdraw with a discretion often mixed with melancholy. Sometimes she would add a few words of warning: 'My little one, if you go out tonight, be sure to wrap up well . . . it's very cold. Take care of him, won't you, Monsieur? He had one of his attacks a little while ago.' His asthma was getting worse and often, although his dress shirt had been prepared and put to air before the log-fire that burned, even in the summer, in the dining room grate (he had a horror of cold underclothes and was always

Continuing the family tradition Marc Porel is a film actor, like his mother Jacqueline, granddaughter of Réjane.

convinced they were damp) he would decide, at the last minute, not to go out after all. On those evenings his dinner would consist of a steaming cup of coffee and he would give his guests a glass of cider—a reminder of La Beauce—'its bubbles clouded the glass and making it very beautiful embroidered its rosy surface with a thousand tiny lights.' Sometimes he dined at Larue's or at Weber's and one might see him arriving in the rue Royale, wearing his fur coat even in Spring and looking deathly pale beneath his black head of hair. At other times, he entertained his friends at the rue de Courcelles. His parents let him play the host and it gave him great pleasure to bring together men like Léon Daudet and Anatole

ALPHONSE DAUDET
EST MORT DANS CETTE MAISON
41
SORTIE
VOITURE
STATIONNER

France who had not been on speaking terms since the Dreyfus Affair. Madame de Noailles, just then at the peak of her young talent, was one of the ornaments of these dinner parties. Montesquiou would come sometimes, and then what care had to be taken with the list of guests! When he was feeling better, Marcel would make excursions to look at trees, or pictures, or beautiful churches. He went to Holland with Bertrand de Fénelon, to Burgundy with Louis d'Albuféra, to Venice with his mother. For him, these were great excursions. In summer when there was a lull between his attacks, he would pay surprise visits to Léon Daudet at Fontainebleau, Madame Alphonse Daudet at Touraine, or to the Finalys or to Madame Straus in Normandy. His future publisher Gaston Gallimard met him for the first time at Bénerville at the house of Louisa de Mornand. Proust had come over on foot from Cabourg. 'It was at this time,' Georges de Lauris tells us, 'that he and some others of us used to go out and visit the churches and the buildings that he loved. We didn't have to worry about him being ready in the morning, for he simply stayed up all night. En route, he would take nothing but coffee, for which he would pay handsomely. We went to Laon, and to Coucy. In spite of his breathlessness and his fatigue, he managed to climb to the platform of the great tower that was later destroyed by the Germans. I remember that he made the ascent leaning on the arm of Bertrand de Fénelon who was singing *The magic of Good Friday* to him, very softly, by way of encouragement. It was, in fact, Good Friday and the fruit trees were in blossom under the morning sun. And I can see Marcel in front of the church at Senlis listening with great attention while Prince Emmanuel Bibesco explained, with great modesty and as if he knew it was impossible to teach Marcel anything, the characteristics of the bell-towers of the Ile-de-France. . . .'

The Proust family moved to 45, rue de Courcelles in 1900, three years later at the time of Robert's marriage, Dr Adrien Proust was photographed with his younger son for the last time. The building has changed but little since then as has the Institute where Proust briefly worked. The winter scene of the quai du Louvre, opposite the Bibliothèque Mazarine painted by Edouard Cortes.

Separations

Around him, his friends were marrying. His brother Robert had married Marthe Dubois-Amiot in 1903, had left the rue de Courcelles and had gone to live in the boulevard Saint-Germain. In 1904, the Duc de Guiche married Elaine Greffulhe, only child of the Comtesse Greffulhe whom Proust used to admire so much and whose photographs he had tried in vain to persuade Montesquiou to give him. *Proust to the Duc de Guiche*: 'I told Madame Greffulhe that you see your marriage (one aspect of it only, of course) as a way of possessing her photograph. She laughed so prettily that I should have liked to have said it to her ten times over. I hope my friendship with you may afford me that privilege.' All his life, Proust attached an extraordinary importance to the acquisition of photographs. In his room he had a whole collection which he used

CICA

BIBLIOTHECA A FVNDATORE MAZARINEA

BIBLIOTHEQUE MAZARINE
INSTITUT DE FRANCE

Jean Béraud . 1889
SEM

Jean Lorrain was a scurrilous columnist, a writer of more than dubious works under the pseudonym of Raitïf de la Bretonne, who published a review in 1897 implying a homosexual relationship between Proust and Lucien Daudet. A duel was fought on 6 February, with no one hurt, and honour undamaged. Jean Béraud (Elstir) whose painting is above, was one of Proust's seconds.

515
Paris
Méprise, ô soldat, l'infâme délateur;
Vois la noble mission confiée à ton honneur.

to show to his friends. He would scrutinise the images with the same attention he gave to hawthorn or to roses, as if he were trying to free some imprisoned spirit from them and extract unspoken confessions. Ten years later he was to write to Simone de Caillavet, daughter of Jeanne Pouquet: 'It would make me so happy if you were to give me your photograph. I will think of you with or without a photograph, but my memory is so blunted by sedatives and has so many gaps, that photographs are very precious to me. I keep them to sustain me and do not look at them too often for fear of diminishing their virtue. . . When I was in love with your

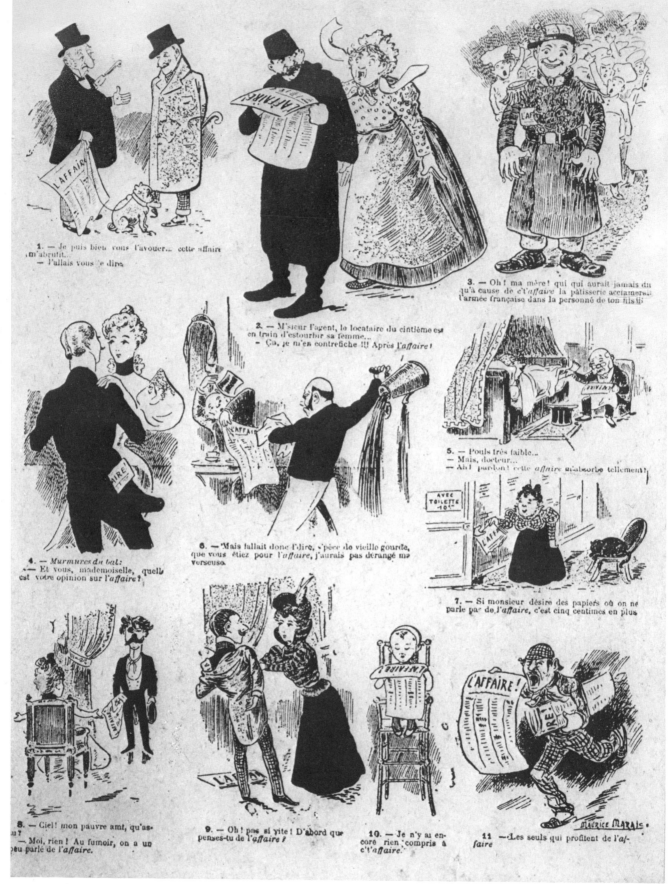

LA SEMAINE DE L'AFFAIRE (1) par Maurice Marais.

1. — Je puis bien vous l'avouer... cette affaire m'abrutit...
— J'allais vous le dire.

2. — M'sieur l'agent, le locataire du cintième est en train d'estourbir sa femme...
— Ça, je m'en contrefiche !!! Après *l'affaire* !

3. — Oh ! ma mère ! qui qui aurait jamais dit qu'à cause de c't'*affaire* la pâtisserie acclamerait l'armée française dans la personnė de ton fils !!!

4. — *Murmures du bal :*
— Et vous, mademoiselle, quelle est votre opinion sur *l'affaire* ?

5. — Pouls très faible...
— Mais, docteur...
— Ah ! pardon ! cette *affaire* m'absorbe tellement !

6. — Mais fallait donc l'dire, s'pèce de vieille gourde, que vous étiez pour *l'affaire*, j'aurais pas dérangé ma verseuse.

7. — Si monsieur désire des papiers où on ne parle pas de *l'affaire*, c'est cinq centimes en plus

8. — Ciel ! mon pauvre ami, qu'as-tu ?
— Moi, rien ! Au fumoir, on a un peu parlé de *l'affaire*.

9. — Oh ! pas si vite ! D'abord que penses-tu de *l'affaire* ?

10. — Je n'y ai encore rien compris à c't'*affaire*.

11 — Les seuls qui profitent de l'*affaire*

The Dreyfus Affair is as much a part of the climate of the book as it was in life. The partisans of both sides were equally vociferous and the affair was everyone's affair for years. Even the Proust family was divided, with the Doctor a convinced anti-Dreyfusard, unlike his wife and sons.

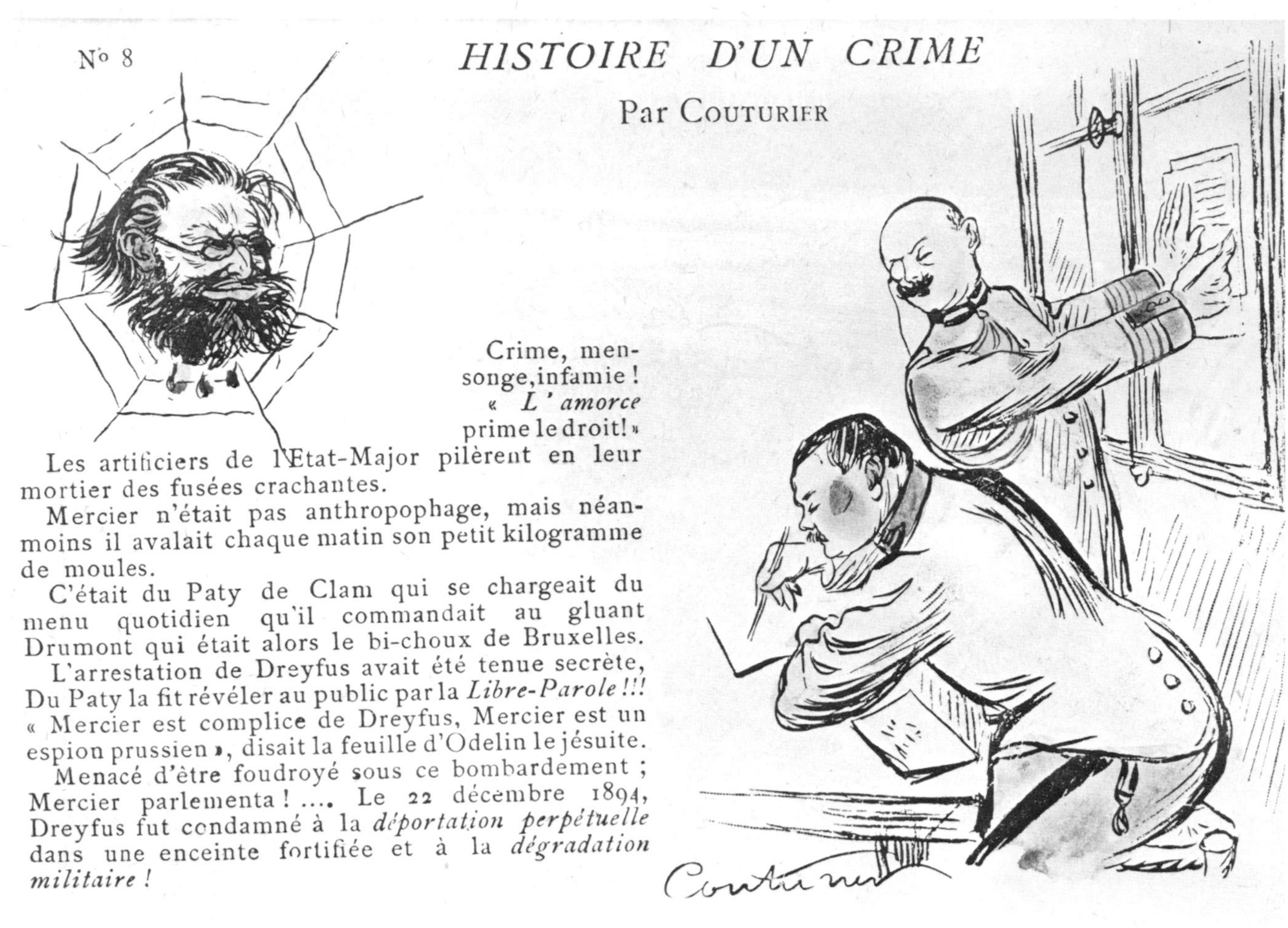
N° 8
HISTOIRE D'UN CRIME
Par COUTURIER
Crime, mensonge, infamie ! « L'amorce prime le droit! »
Les artificiers de l'Etat-Major pilèrent en leur mortier des fusées crachantes.
Mercier n'était pas anthropophage, mais néanmoins il avalait chaque matin son petit kilogramme de moules.
C'était du Paty de Clam qui se chargeait du menu quotidien qu'il commandait au gluant Drumont qui était alors le bi-choux de Bruxelles.
L'arrestation de Dreyfus avait été tenue secrète, Du Paty la fit révéler au public par la *Libre-Parole* !!! « Mercier est complice de Dreyfus, Mercier est un espion prussien », disait la feuille d'Odelin le jésuite.
Menacé d'être foudroyé sous ce bombardement ; Mercier parlementa ! .... Le 22 décembre 1894, Dreyfus fut condamné à la *déportation perpétuelle* dans une enceinte fortifiée et à la *dégradation militaire* !
Couturier

mother, I went to tremendous lengths to obtain her photograph. But all to no avail. I still receive cards on New Year's Day from all sorts of people in Périgourd with whom I became involved with the sole object of obtaining that photograph. . . .' The little domestic happiness he had of his own was rapidly disintegrating. Towards the end of 1903, his father had a stroke while he was at work. Marcel dedicated his translation of the *Bible of Amiens* to him: 'To the memory of my father, struck down at work, 24th November 1903, died 26th November, this translation is affectionately dedicated.' Madame Proust, who had been a devoted wife, never recovered from the shock. Henceforth, she lived only for her mourning, which she cultivated with an astonishing number of anniversaries and mortifications. As far as he could, during the years 1904 and 1905, Proust lived with and for his mother. In August 1905, he took her to Evian where she became seriously ill with uraemia. 'She is in Paris now,' he wrote to Montesquiou, 'in a state that torments me and makes me wretched.' It is probable that the very

A few moments after being photographed outside the Palais de Justice during the Dreyfus trial, Zola, Clemenceau, and Labori's taxi was attacked by anti-Dreyfusards. The three men barely escaped the violence of the mob.

beautiful descriptions of the death of the grandmother in *Côté de Guermantes* are based on scenes he lived through himself. There were a few days of apparent improvement. *Proust to Montesquiou*: 'Whatever hope the slight improvement of these last few days has given us (and I cannot tell you how sweet this word "hope" is to me, it makes it possible for me to go on living), the upward struggle out of the abyss will be so long that the progress of each day, if God wills that it continue, will be imperceptible. Since you have been kind enough to be concerned for my distress, I will write and tell you if there is any definite news to deliver us from our torments. But do not trouble to reply. I cannot tell you how I have suffered . . . She knows that I am incapable of living without her and am so defenceless in this life and if she felt, and I am wretched for I fear she has done so, that she were going to leave me for ever, then she must have experienced such moments of terrible anxiety that, to imagine them, is hell for me.' She died and Marcel's despair aroused deep compassion in his friends. Reynaldo

180. — Exposition Universelle. Château d'Eau. Palais d'Electricité.

Hahn wrote in his *Diary*: 'I have thought a long time about Marcel and about his loneliness. I shall always remember him at his Mother's death-bed, weeping and smiling at the body through his tears.' To Laure Hayman, Proust wrote: 'And now my heart is empty, and my room is empty and my life. . . .' To Montesquiou: 'I have lost her, I have seen her suffer, I believe she knew that she was leaving me and that she could no longer advise me and it

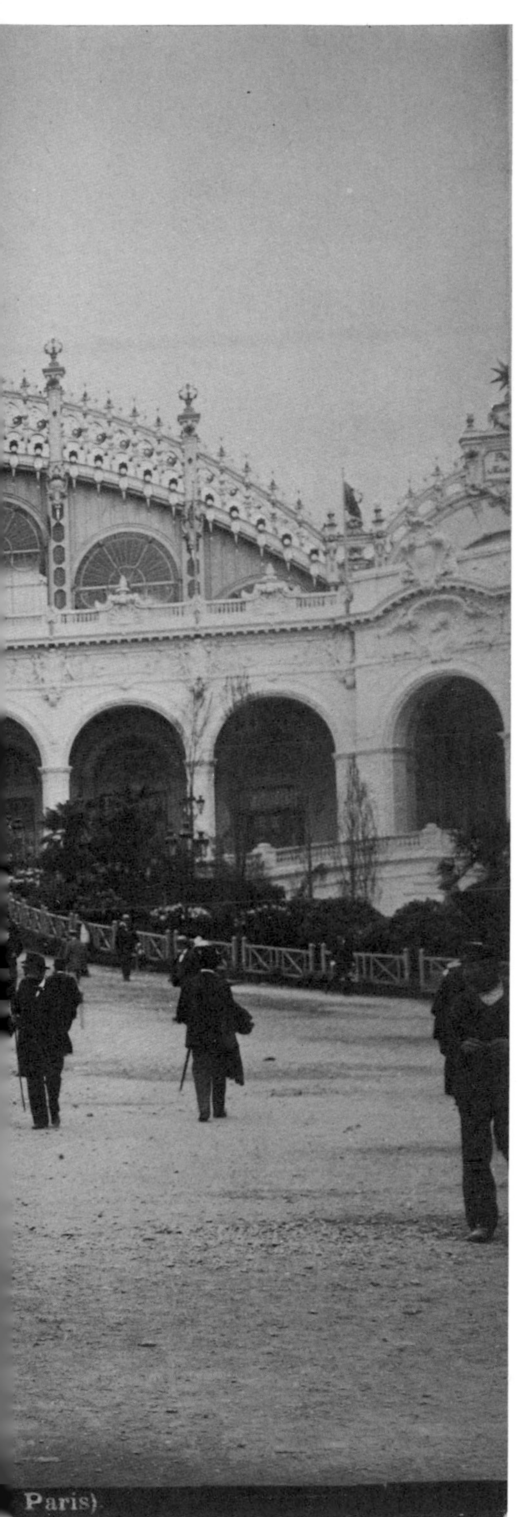

The Great Exposition of 1900 was remarkable in its time for many things, not the least of them its banality and hideousness. Few mementoes remain except the place name for the flea-market, Village Suisse. The Trocadero came down in the 1930s and the great wheel which stood in the Champs de Mars was a landmark until 1922.

tortured her; I feel that, with my poor health, I was the sorrow and the worry of her life. . . .' He remained for fifteen months in the rue de Courcelles where his parents had died, until the lease ran out. Then, towards the end of 1906, he moved to a house at 102, boulevard Haussmann which belonged to the widow of his uncle, the magistrate Georges Weil. *Marcel Proust to Madame Catusse*: 'I could not bring myself to live, without a period of transition, in a house that my mother never knew and so for this year I have sub-let my uncle's old apartment in the house at 102, boulevard Haussmann where mother and I often used to dine, where I saw my uncle die in the very room that I shall have. Were it not for these memories, all the other things—the gilt decorations on the pink walls, the dust of the neighbourhood, the incessant noise and the trees that lean against the very windows—I would never have chosen it!'

In this new room, Marcel insisted that his bed, flanked by the little table he called his 'long boat' and which held books, papers, fountain pens and the materials for his fumigations, should be placed exactly as it had been in the boulevard Malesherbes and the rue de Courcelles 'so that he had a diagonal view of his guests entering the room, and the daylight was to the left of him—when it was allowed in at all—as was also the warmth of the fire which was always too much or too little to please him. . . .' The reading matter on his 'long boat' had nearly always been borrowed from his friends. When the old home had been packed up, the family library was buried underneath the furniture, chandeliers and carpets of which these were far too many for the smaller apartment—so Marcel was unable to get at any of his own books. Thus he would lend a Sainte-Beuve or a Mérimée he had just bought to Georges de Lauris, saying: 'Keep it, if I need it I'll ask you for it. It will only get lost in my place. . . .' For Marcel, the move had been an uprooting and a tragedy. As always, he had consulted his friends. Madame de Noailles had been called to the telephone one evening to speak to the wine waiter at the Hôtel des Réservoirs at Versailles who enquired with a scrupulous simplicity 'if she would advise Monsieur Proust to rent the apartment in the boulevard Haussmann'.

Madame Catusse was another who received innumerable letters: 'Do you think the furniture from Mama's room (the blue one) would be too dusty, or do you think it would do for my room? Do you think it's pretty? Would you prefer it for a small drawing room like mine rather than the furniture from Papa's study in the rue de Courcelles? . . .'

The Cork-lined Room

Marcel had other reasons for fussing over thesc details. He had just begun his great work. No one knew then, not even he, that generation after generation would know this work as *A la recherche du temps perdu*; it was going to tax him to the limit. Would he have the strength to finish it? Always anxious about noise disturbing his sleep, he finally hit upon a solution: to have his room entirely lined with cork. It was thus between four walls padded with cork and proof against outside noise that he wrote his great book. Around him were his *Notebooks*, school exercise-books, covered in black moleskin, from which he cut passages here and there to paste into the final manuscript. The room was full of the yellow vapours of his fumigations and impregnated with their acrid smell. Through the fog, one could distinguish Marcel, pale, a little puffy about the face, his eyes shining across the haze, dressed in a light shirt and innumerable threadbare and scorched pullovers one on top of the other. Ramon Fernandez described one of his nocturnal visits to the boulevard Haussmann and Proust's voice, 'that miraculous voice, discreet, vague, abstracted, punctuated and muffled that seemed to form its sounds beyond the teeth or the lips or even the throat in some mysterious regions of his very intelligence . . . His splendid eyes seemed to fix themselves on the furniture, on the materials or the knick-knacks: he seemed to be breathing in, through every pore of his body, the reality contained in the room, in that moment, even in me; and the kind of ecstasy that lit up his face was like that of a medium receiving invisible messages from physical objects. He was very fulsome in his expressions of admiration which I did not take as flattery since, wherever he looked, he created a masterpiece. . . .' Each specialist was consulted on his particular subject, Reynaldo Hahn on music, Jean-Louis Vaudoyer on painting, the Daudet family on flowers. In each case, he wanted technical terms 'so that a musician, a gardener, a painter or a doctor might think, when he read his work, that Proust had devoted

Prince Antoine Bibesco (recently, and in uniform during the first World War) and his brother Emmanuel met Proust in 1899 and remained devoted friends throughout their lives. They were passionate amateurs of gothic architecture, and with Proust, Robert de Billy and Bertrand de Fénelon made numerous pilgrimages to the famous cathedrals of France. It was largely due to their influence that Proust was able to see these masterpieces for himself rather than through Ruskin's worshipful eyes. They were also cousins of Anna de Noailles.

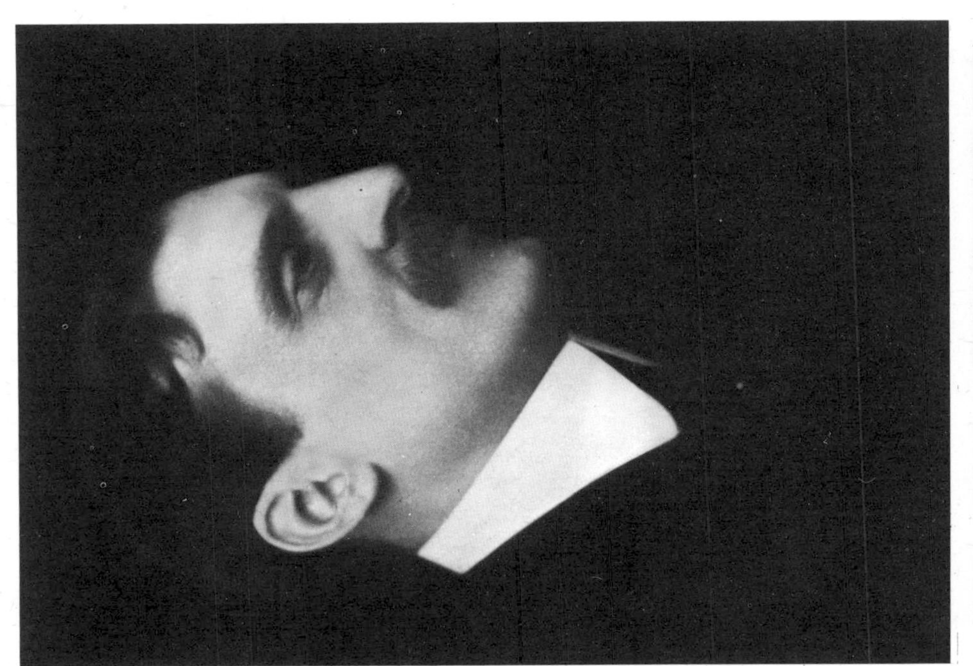

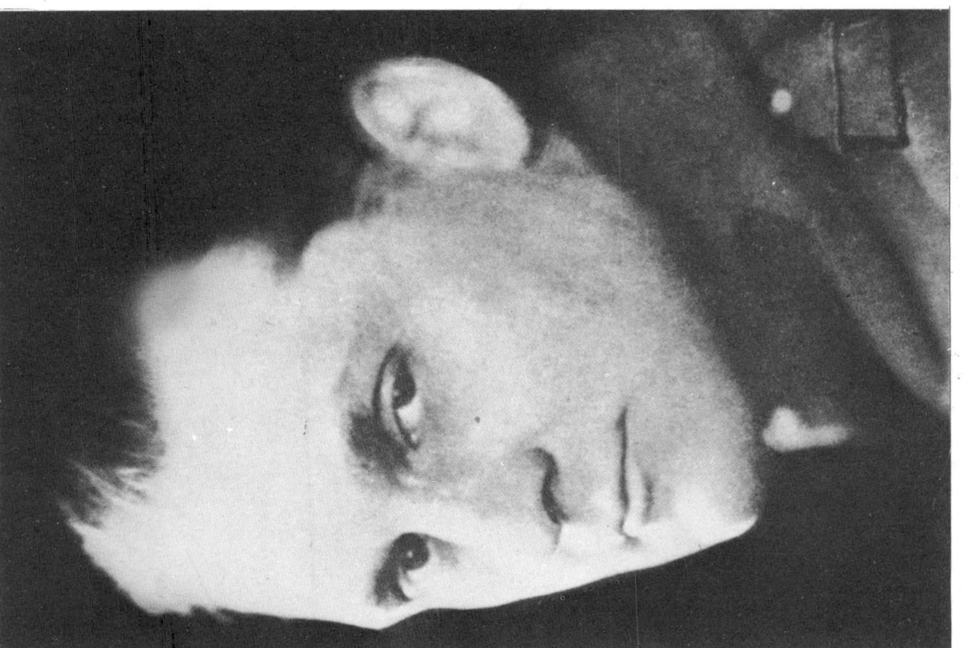

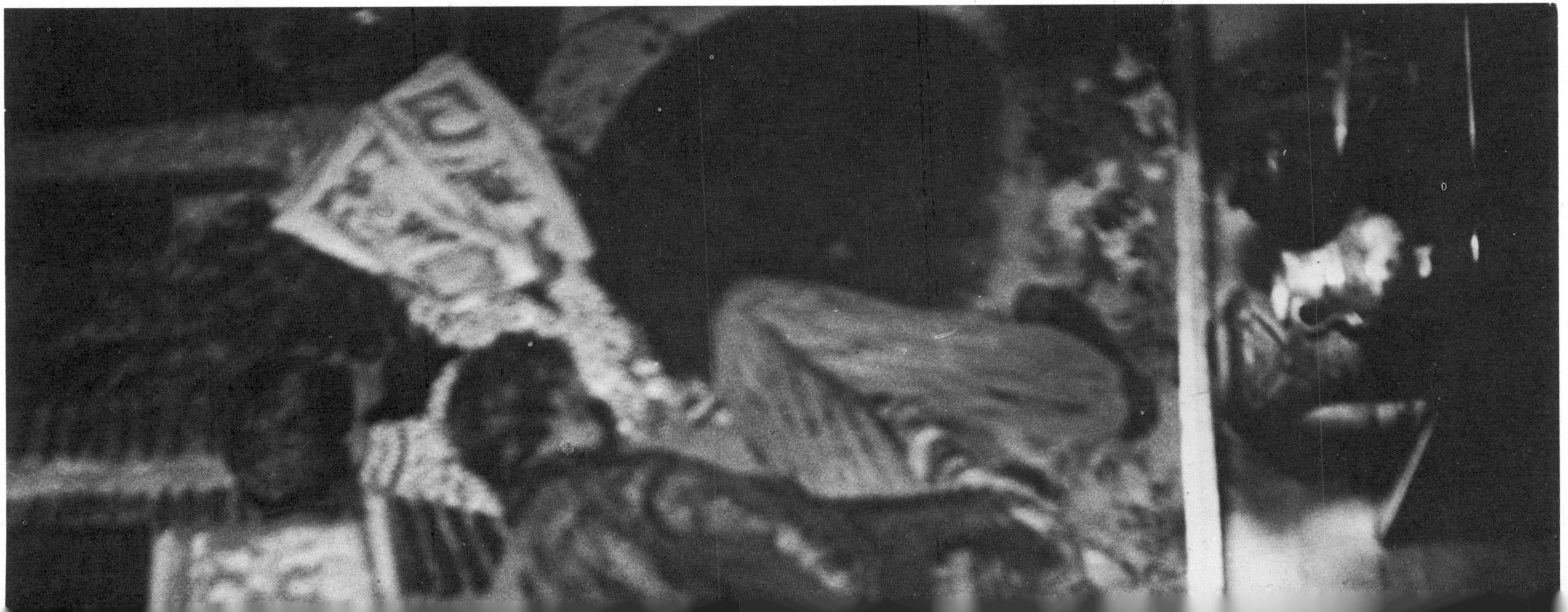

The Princesse Marthe Bibesco, née Lahovary, was another cousin. She was a stunningly beautiful young woman when she arrived in Paris in 1908. Yet despite Proust's instant admiration for her and the opportunities they frequently had to become friends she never really became close to him until the last months of his life. However she has written beautifully about Proust and the effect his life and work had upon her own. The two photographs are separated by forty-five years.

The painting of the Pré Catelan in the Bois de Boulogne dates from about 1910 and the photograph was taken in 1972.

338 PARIS. — Le Bois de Boulogne. — Les Acacias — LL.

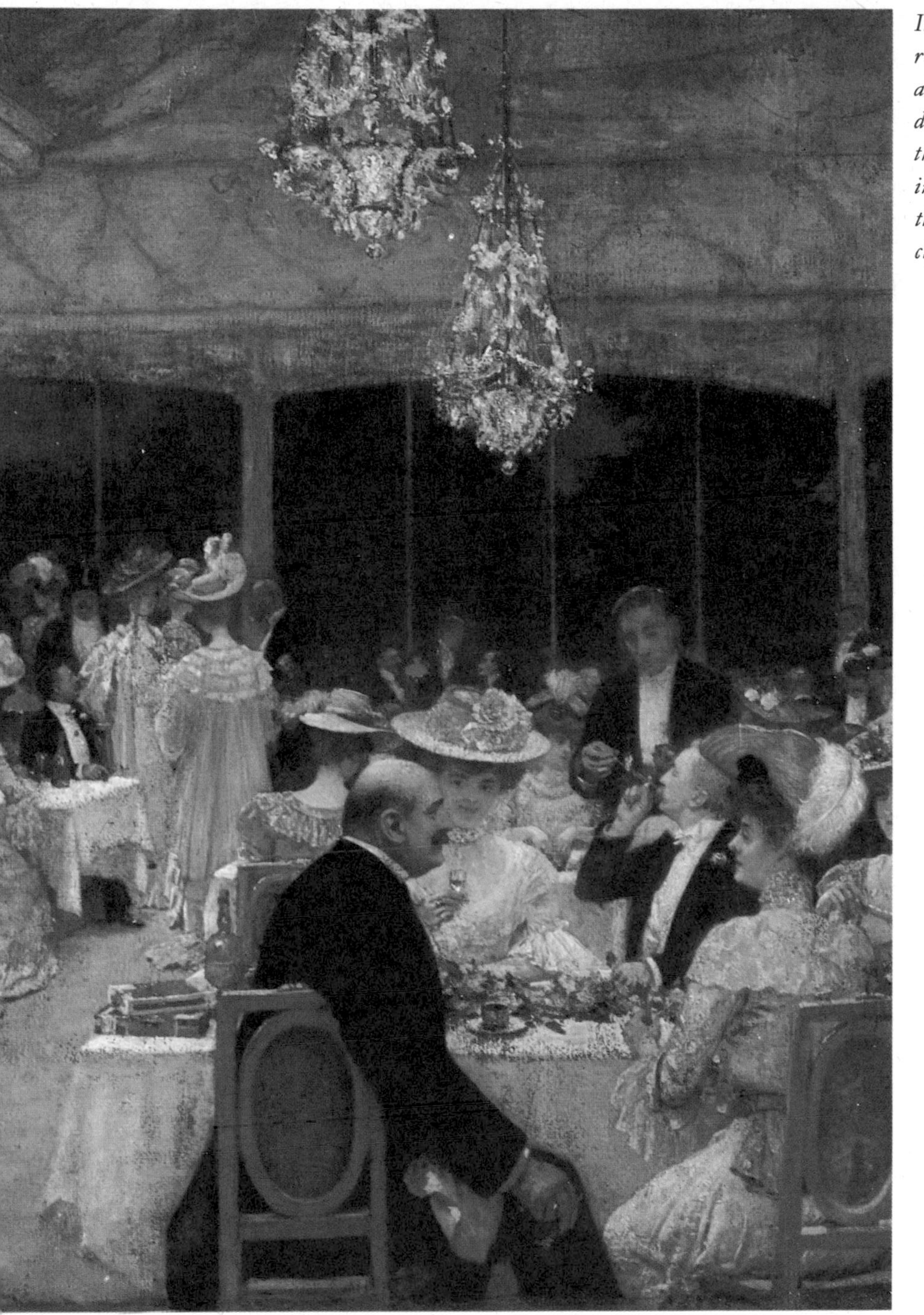

In the Bois de Boulogne, the interior of the restaurant at Armenonville, and the avenue along which the aged, ill, Baron de Charlus was wheeled and, still with the longings of youth, contemplated impossible pleasures. Boni de Castellane, the impulsive spendthrift, is having his cigar lighted.

Places of assignation, also in the Bois,
sought out by Charlus, from the Pré Catelan . . . .

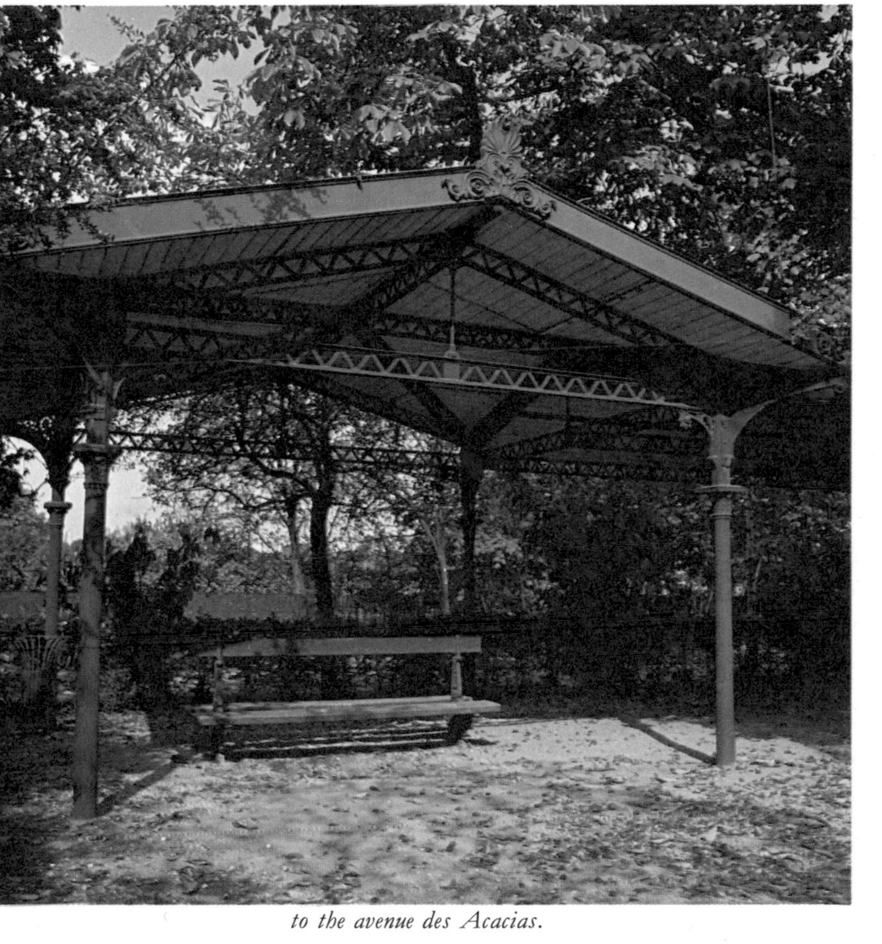

to the avenue des Acacias.

The Grande Cascade

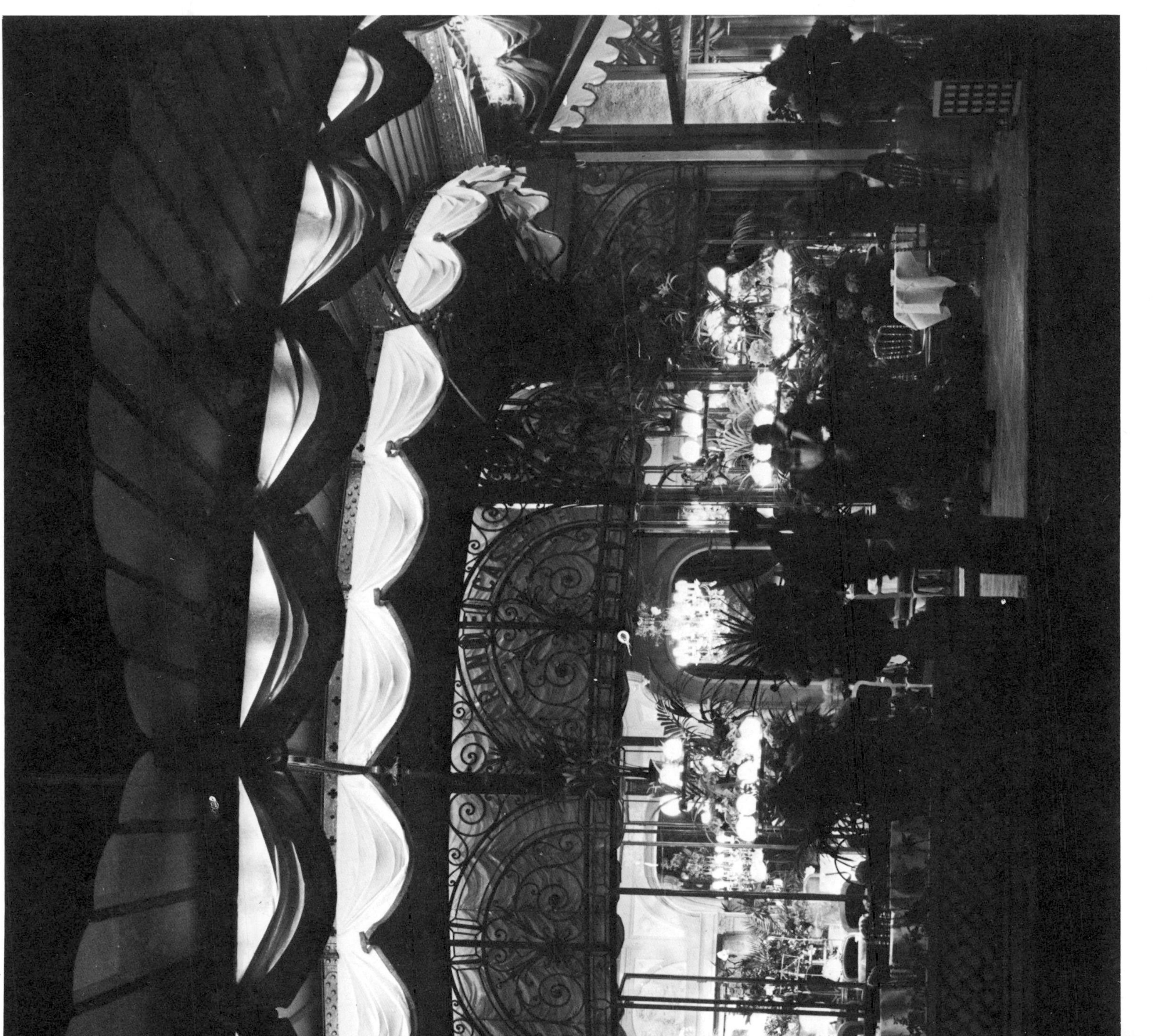

Ten years before the first World War—the avenue des Acacias

years to music or to gardening, to painting or to medicine'. 'We did the best we could,' said Lucien Daudet 'to supply him with information, without knowing why it was necessary, on the kind of cakes one might find, after mass on a Sunday, at the bakers in such and such a provincial town, or on shrubs that are in bloom at the same time as hawthorn and lilac, or the flower that is not exactly a hyacinth but has the same shape, and the same use, etc. . . .' He asked his women friends for help on more feminine matters. *Proust to Madame Gaston de Caillavet*: 'Could you by any chance give me one or two details about clothes, for the book I am writing? (Please don't think that was why I telephoned you the other day; I wasn't thinking of that, I simply wanted to see you). . . .' There

followed urgent questions on the dress that Madame Greffulhe had worn at an Italian production by the Theatre of Monte Carlo 'in a very dark box near the stage about two months ago.' (The details were used to dress the Princesse de Guermantes at the Opera.) He would have liked to have seen dresses and hats his friends had worn twenty years before and was indignant to find they had not kept them. 'My dear Marcel, that hat is twenty years old; I haven't got it now.' 'It's not possible, Madame. You don't *want* to show it to me. You have it and you just want to vex me. I shall be very hurt indeed. . . .' One evening, at half past eleven, he arrived at the house of his friends, the Caillavets, whom he had not seen for some time. 'Are Monsieur and Madame in bed? Could they see me?' Of

The Bois

course they could see him. 'Madame, would you like to make me very, very happy? I haven't seen your daughter for such a long time. I may never be here again . . . and it's not very likely that you'll ever bring her to my house! By the time she's old enough to go to a ball I shan't be going out any longer; I am so ill. So, please, Madame, I beg you to let me see Mademoiselle Simone now.' 'But, Marcel, she went to bed long ago.'

'Madame, I implore you, go and see, if she's not asleep, explain to her. . . .'

Simone came down and met the strange visitor. What was he looking for in her? For details that he needed on the portrait of Mademoiselle de Saint-Loup, daughter of a woman the Narrator had once loved. If he were well enough, he would travel further

afield in search of images of the past. 'I go out now and then and it's usually to see the hawthorn or the finery of three apple trees in their ballgowns under a grey sky.' When his attacks were too frequent he did not even risk looking through his window at the chestnut-trees on the street, and a whole autumn passed without him seeing its colours. When the holiday season came round, he would indulge in a terrifying but harmless orgy of train times and would plan a thousand itineraries of which he would dream between two and six o'clock in the morning, lying on his sofa. If, on the other hand, he were slightly better, he might venture forth. 'The exceptions to the rule are the fairy-tales of life,' he would say. He called on the Duchesse de Clermont-Tonnerre one evening at Glisolles when he was 'doing Normandy' in a taxi and admiring

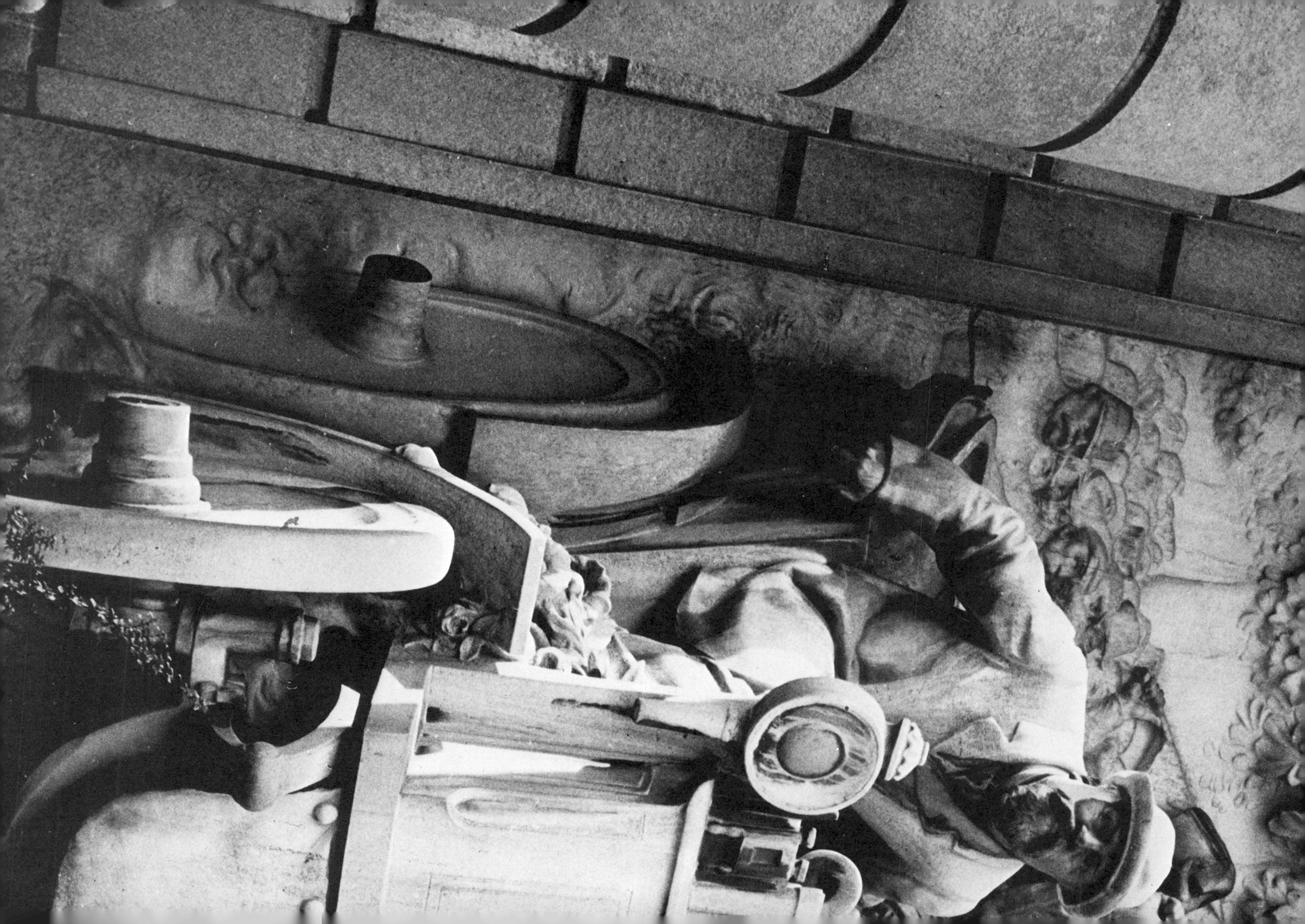

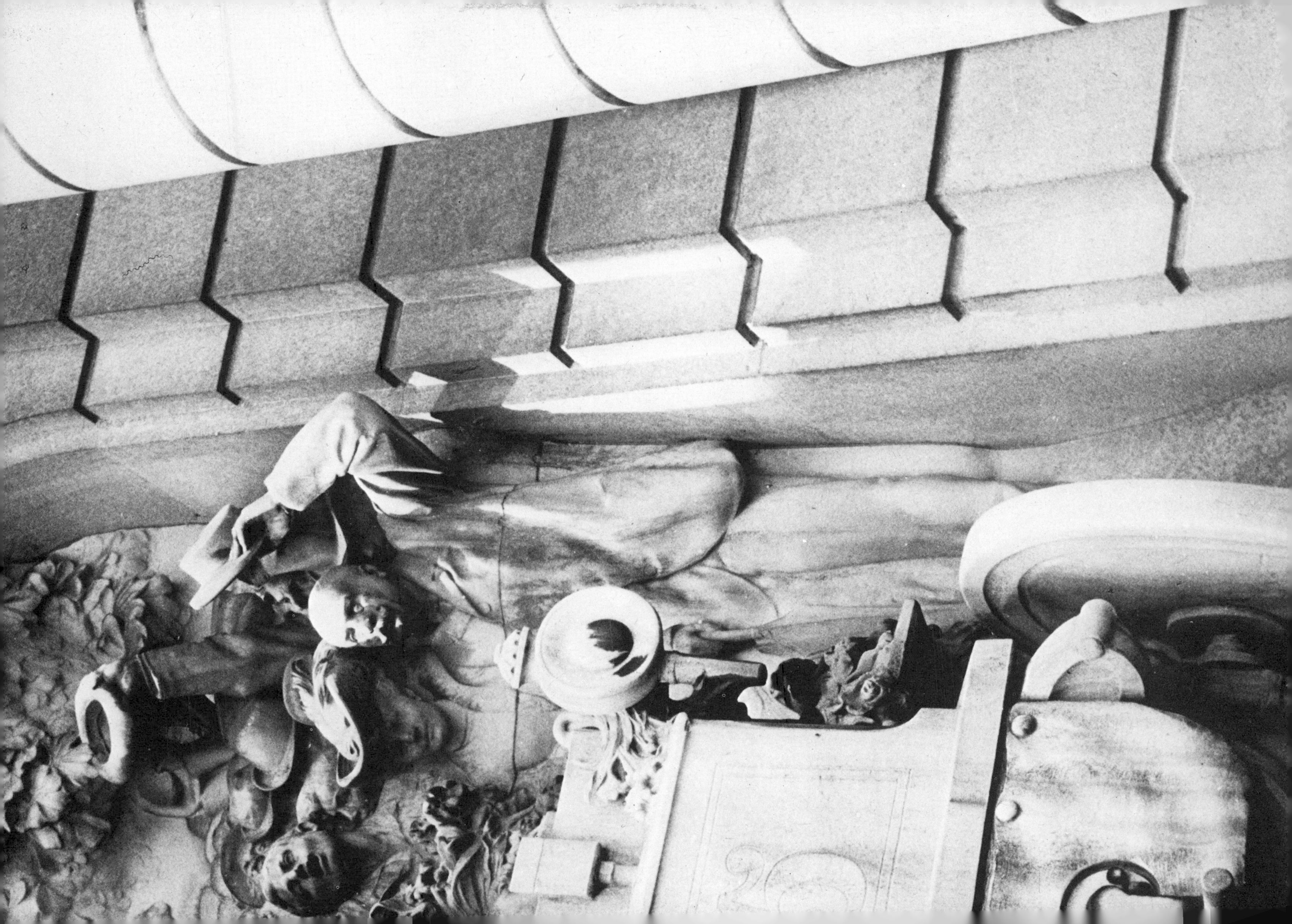

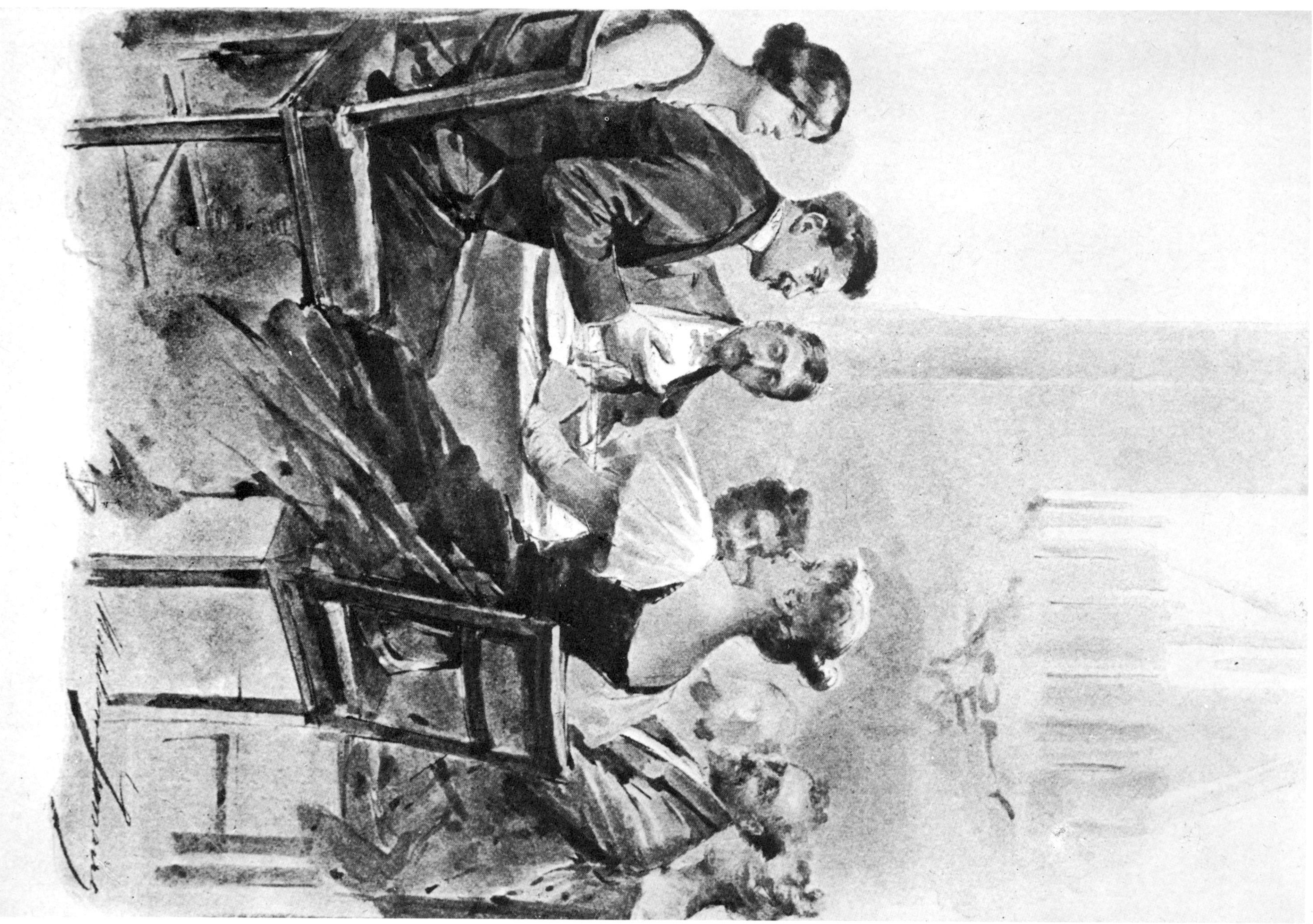

The first venture into literature which Proust made was entitled Les Jours et les Plaisirs, *he had it sponsored by way of an introduction through his friendship with Mme de Caillavet, by Anatole France and illustrated by Madeleine Lemaire.*

the flowers through tightly-closed windows. 'We shone the head-lamps on the rose-walks and the roses looked like beautiful women we had torn from sleep.' He was on his way to see 'the windows at Evreux which somehow managed to snatch jewels of light from the opaque indifference of a rainy sky, and thus perform a miracle worthy of being recorded in the Cathedral among the many others that are much less interesting.' He fortified himself for these trips exclusively on café au lait and thanked his hostess 'for having guided his steps, that faltered from too much caffeine, on these nocturnal wanderings.' In 1910, he dreamed of a trip to Pontigny: 'Do you know the lay Abbey of Paul Desjardins at Pontigny? If I were ever well enough for such an uncomfortable journey, that is what would tempt me.'

But above all and as often as he could, he went to Cabourg to see more clearly the ghosts of Balbec and *l'Ombre des jeunes filles en fleurs*. He had to have three rooms in the hotel (to be certain of avoiding noisy neighbours), one of which was for Félicie. 'Do you think perhaps I am a little ridiculous to bring my ancient cook to an hotel?' The suite had to be cheerful, and comfortable *with no footsteps overhead*. If necessary, he rented the room above his own. All day, he would remain closeted in his room, working or interrogating the servants who brought him little snippets of information on the other guests or the staff. When the sun had gone down and his old enemy, the Day, had been routed, he would come downstairs, bearing a parasol and, standing for a moment on the door-step like some night bird emerging from its sombre hiding place at dusk, would reassure himself that the sky was not merely clouded over and that there would be no offensive return of the daylight. Later, ensconced at a big table in the dining room he would play the host, very simply and with great charm and, frozen to the bone, would offer champagne to anyone who cared to join him.

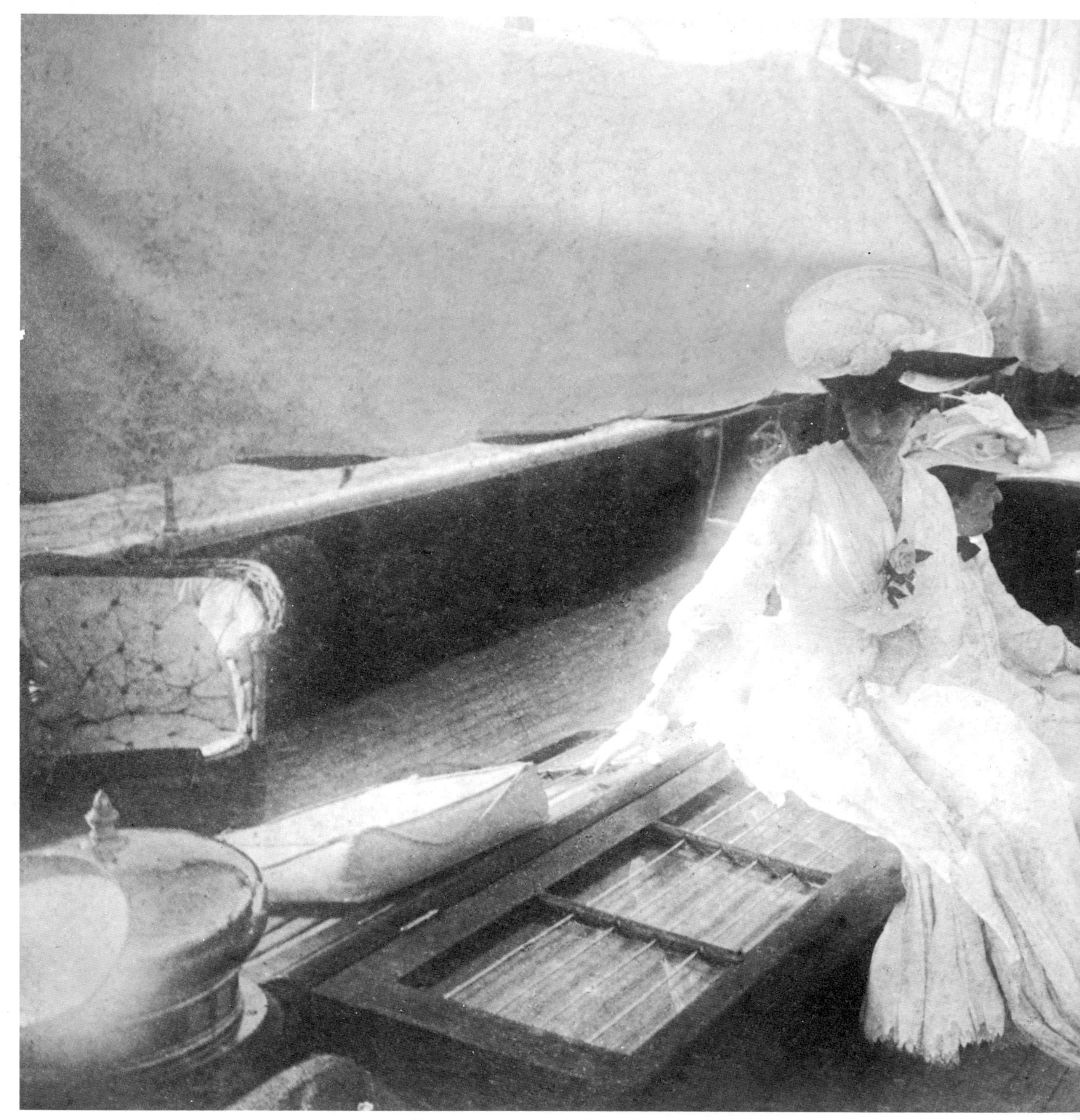

In Paris, he still went to some of the salons, in pursuit of one or other of his characters, but he always arrived so late that, when they saw him people would cry 'Marcel! its two o'clock in the morning' and take to their heels. Such was the case of Anatole France on Madame Arman de Caillavet's 'Wednesdays'.

When Proust entertained his friends now, it was no longer in his own home but in a restaurant and most frequently at the Ritz

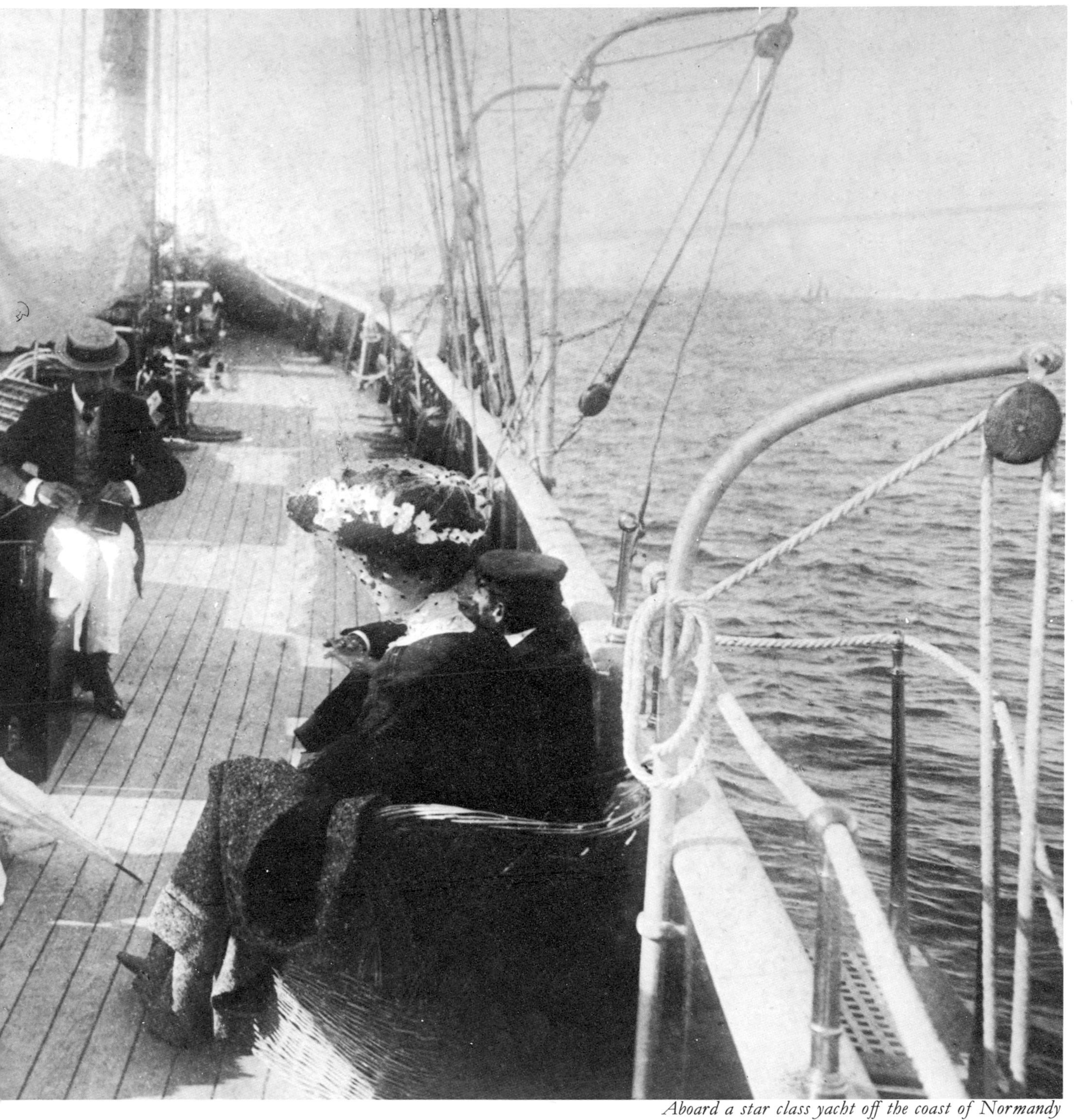

Aboard a star class yacht off the coast of Normandy

whose maître d'hôtel, Olivier Dabescat, delighted him, with his air of discreet distinction, his officious dignity and his certain knowledge of what was correct. A dinner for Calmette, the editor of *Figaro*, who welcomed his articles with open arms, was in Proust's eyes an event necessitating lengthy letters to Madame Straus and telephone calls (which, however, he did not make himself) to each of the guests: to Gabriel Fauré, who was going to

play for them, as Reynaldo was in London singing before King Edward VII and Queen Alexandra. And, could one invite Monsieur Joseph Reinach at the same time as the Duc de Clermont-Tonnerre? And what was the order of precedence between Fauré 'who is no longer young; Calmette, for whom I am giving the dinner; Béraud, who is very easily offended; Monsieur de Clermont-Tonnerre who is younger but *is* in direct line from Charlemagne; and what about the foreigners? . . .' Eventually the dinner took place in a room at the Ritz with cerise brocade curtain and gilt furniture. 'The two Lapps muffled in furs' surprised many in this setting—they were Proust and Madame de Noailles. Risler, engaged at the last moment,

Venice, May 1900

played Wagnerian overtures. When dinner was over and it was time to do the tipping, Proust wanted to give three hundred francs to Olivier but his guests fell upon him and tried to persuade him to be a little less generous. Needless to say, he paid no heed to them. But Cabourg, the Ritz and his nocturnal wandering were only a kind of reconnoitering to gather information on the enemy, the outside world. Proust's real life, during these years of work, was lived in bed where he wrote, surrounded by what Félicie, inherited from Madame Proust (Françoise of the novel) called 'his little bits of paper', that is to say his *Memoranda*, his *Notebooks* and his innumerable photographs. The papers got torn here and there, as

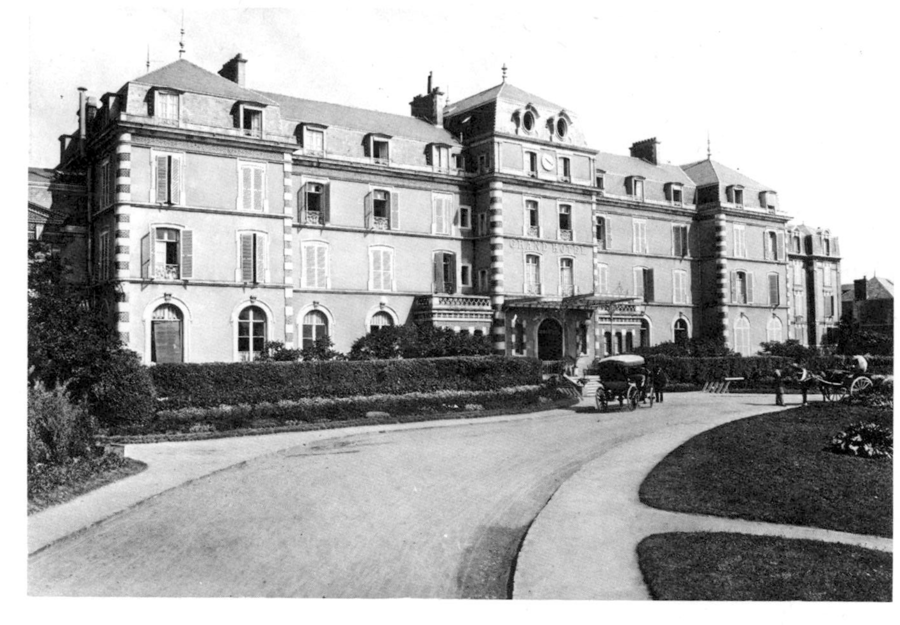

The scene at Cabourg, with the Grand Hôtel in which Proust stayed in 1907 complaining of the great vulgarity of the guests.

the fragments that were going to build up the most beautiful book in the world were being stuck, the one on top of the other. 'It's all moth-eaten,' Félicie would say. 'Look, here's a bit of a page that's like lace, isn't it a shame now. . . .' And examining it like a tailor, she would add, 'I don't think I can do anything about that piece, it's too far gone.' But nothing was ever too far gone, and slowly, like Françoise's *boeuf à la mode,* the work for which Proust was literally going to give his life was being done.

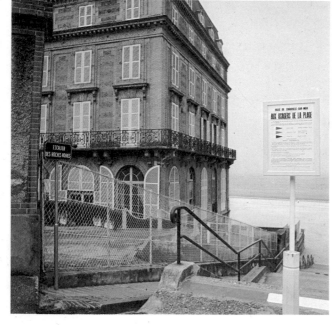

Trouville today and as painted by Monet

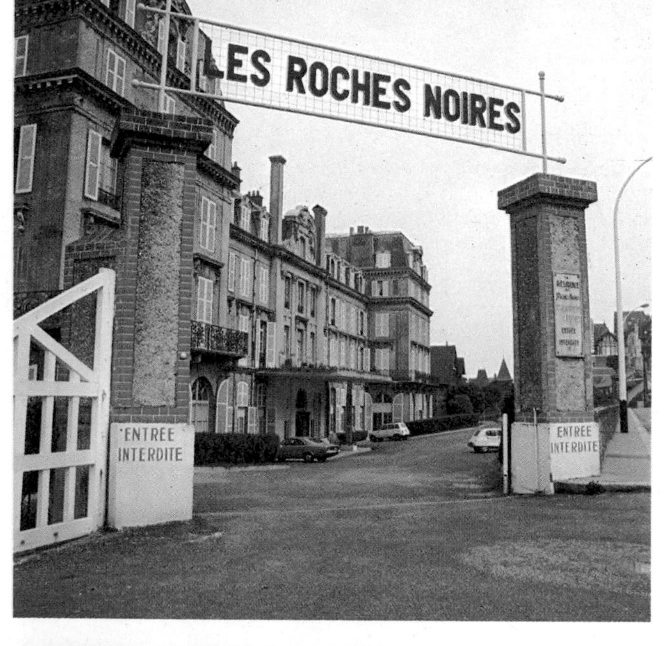

Les Frémonts, which was owned by the family Finaly (who become Bloch), like Mme Straus's villa, la manoir de la Cour Brulée, was near Trouville where so many people foregathered during the summer months and became transformed, in part, into la Raspalière. It was in her mulberry garden that Proust so liked to be photographed.

The duel between Proust and Lorrain was held in the Meudon countryside house la Tour Villebon. This lovely 17th and 18th century home, once belonging to the Hugo family is now abandoned.

In Dives, a town famous for its 15th and 16th century buildings, in an area renowned for its beauty is the old William the Conqueror Inn, now, after so many years closed.

Inspirations for place names. All that remains of the château of Glisolles is a memory kept alive by the road sign.

30. GLISOLLES — Le Château, construit en 1753

The Abbey for Men, St Etienne, founded in Caen in 1066 by William the Conqueror, is one of the noblest simple unadorned masterpieces of Romanesque architecture in Normandy.

'Mme de Villeparisis, seeing how much I loved churches, promised that we would go to see one here, or one there, but that above all we must see the building at Carqueville (Criqueboeuf) completely hidden beneath its ancient ivy, she said with a gentle movement of her hand which seemed to envelope the invisible and delicate façade in a beautiful leafiness.'

Albertine is described amongst just such a group as in Prinet's painting. Of all the characters in the book the components of her make-up are the most complex, wrought of those with whom Proust was emotionally involved both in happiness and misery: his chauffeurs Albert Nahamis and Alfred Agostinelli as well as Henri Rochat, Lousia de Mornand, Marie Finaly, Hélène d'Ideville and Colette d'Alton.

It was a real Albertine who sent this post card from Cabourg in August, 1905.

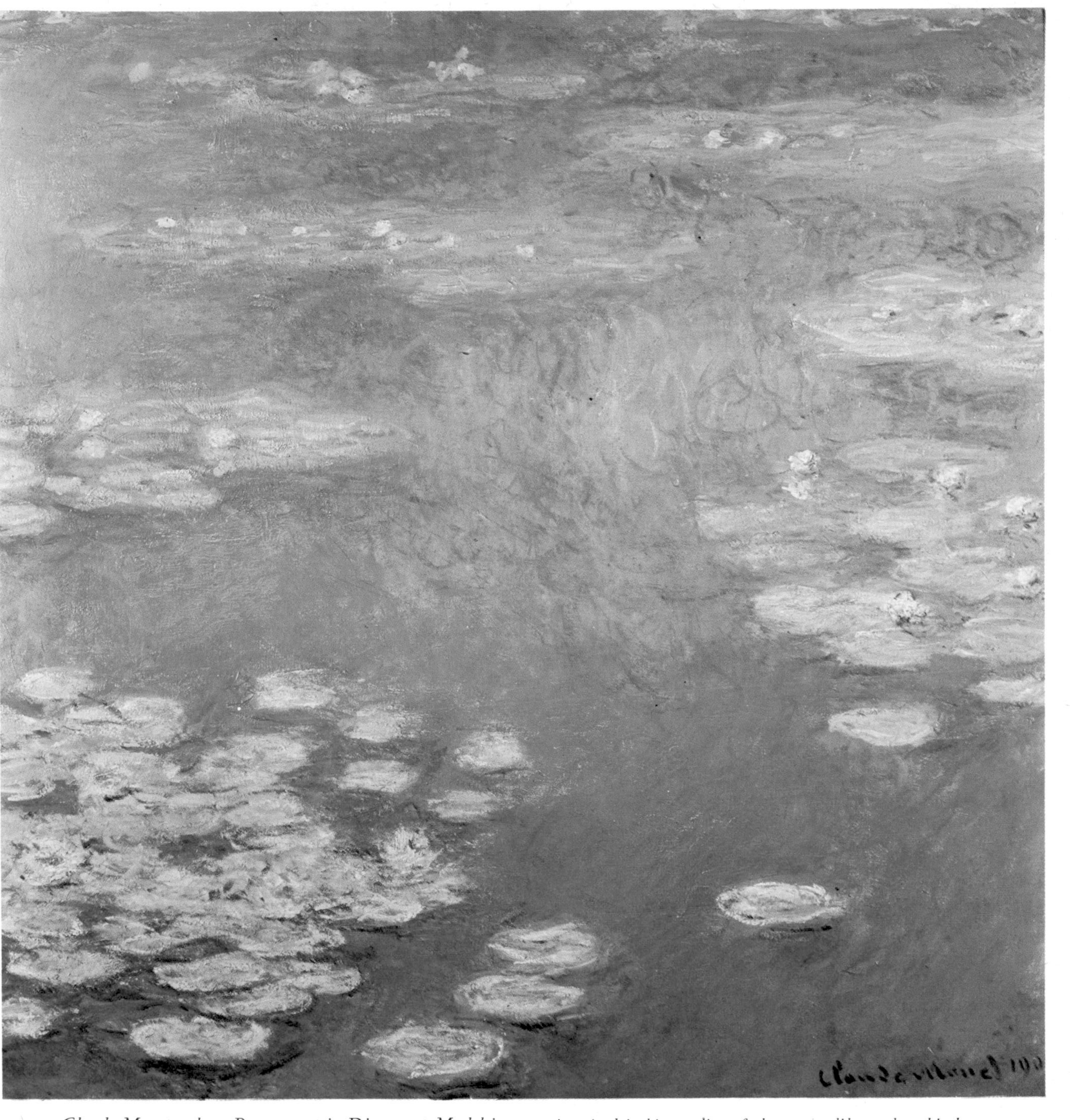

Claude Monet, whom Proust met in Dieppe at Madeleine Lemaire's and whose painting of Impression of a Sunrise *gave the name to an art movement. The style of Monet's work, best epitomised in his studies of the water lily pool at his home, the subtle fusions of light and water and land are described in Elstir's atmospheric subaqueous paintings of harbour scenes.*

The creation of Elstir: the painter is partly made of Manet, here drawn by another, Degas.

The subtleties to be found in the canvases of Le Sidaner, whose self portrait is opposite, are echoed in Elstir's technique.

Keys

On the subject of the 'keys' to his work, one must first quote what Proust had to say on the subject. This is contained in the

long dedication of *Côté de chez Swann* to Jacques de Lacretelle, who had put various pertinent questions to him on the subject. 'There are no keys to the characters in this novel, or rather there are eight or ten to each one . . . In the case of Madame Swann, when she is walking near the Tir aux Pigeons, just for a second I had in mind a ravishingly beautiful cocotte of those days, who was called Clomesnil. I can show you photographs of her. But it is at that moment

Degas and his housekeeper in a self-portrait photograph at the time the artist was friendly with Mme Straus and Charles Haas.

only that Madame Swann resembles her. I say it again, the characters are entirely imaginary and there is no key. . . .'

The portrait of Madame de Chevigné, in *Les Plaisirs et les Jours*, with its bird-like profile and hoarse voice, provides the temporal and real framework of the Duchesse. The very lovely Comtesse Greffulhe lent much to the Princesse de Guermantes. Charlus is not Robert de Montesquiou but his dramatic style of talking and the picturesque harshness of his pride were taken straight from Proust's own imitations of the poet while, physically, Charlus resembled a certain Baron Doazan, a cousin of Madame Aubernon, who was 'rather the same type'.

It has often been said that Swann was Charles Haas, the son of a stockbroker, and was 'made much of in the very best salons, on account of his elegance, his taste and his erudition.' He was a member of the Jockey Club, favourite of the Greffulhes, friend of the Prince of Wales and of the Comte de Paris, and like Swann, had red hair cropped short in the style of the actor, Bressant. Elisabeth de Gramont makes the apt and curious comment that there could be an elegant similarity between Haas, in German, meaning *hare* and Swann, in English, meaning *cygne*. Undoubtedly Haas made a contribution to the character of Swann but his own erudition, which was superficial, had to be complemented by that of another Israelite, Charles Ephrussi, founder of the *Gazette des Beaux-Arts*. However, Swann is primarily an incarnation of Proust himself, which becomes quite obvious in the versions of the *Notebooks*, where the young Swann is made the hero of adventures which later are given to the Narrator.

It has been written a hundred times that Bergotte was Anatole France and there is no doubt that, in certain passages, Bergotte is very much like France. Bergotte's little black beard, his 'snail's-shell' nose and his style of writing all come from Anatole France as do the 'rare, almost archaic phrases which he loved to use at certain moments when some hidden flow of music, some interior prelude uplifted his style.' It was at moments like these that Bergotte would talk of 'the vain dream of life', of 'the unending stream of beautiful appearances', of 'the sweet and sterile torment of

Like Mme Elstir, the beautiful wife of Helleu, Gabrielle in the book, was a woman of fulsome charms, but not accepted as freely in cosmopolitan society.

But above all the physical make-up of Elstir—'in evening dress in his own drawing room' and 'in a frock coat and top-hat at a regatta' a man with a sunken face, black bearded and always dressed in that sombre colour are Helleu. The painter's daughter remembers an evening in 1918 when a chauffeur arrived with an enormous basket of flowers saying that Monsieur Proust regrets calling so unexpectedly but begs leave to ask if he might come up.
A few minutes later swathed in his great fur coat he entered the apartment and took the artist's hands in his saying 'Good evening Monsieur Elstir.'

Mme Howard-Johnston, who signs her painting with her maiden name of Pauline Helleu, lives in the same apartment as her parents did 60 years ago. Among the Proust mementoes is a pair of bronze elephants from his bedroom the writer gave to Helleu.

understanding and loving', of 'the moving effigies that ennoble the charming and venerable façades of our cathedrals for all time', that he could voice 'a philosophy, new to me, full of marvellous images that seemed to have awakened the sound of harp that rose to the heavens and which gave to these images a touch of the sublime.' This certainly was France, but Bergotte is also Renan when, coming across the name of a famous cathedral, he would interrupt his flow and 'in *an* invocation, an apostrophe, a lengthy prayer, would give a free outlet to that effluence which in the earlier volumes remained buried beneath the form of his prose. . . .' But here, yet again, Bergotte is Proust himself and the description of Bergotte's death is based on an attack of indigestion Marcel experienced one day when he was visiting an exhibition of Dutch paintings at the *Jeu de Paume* with Jean-Louis Vaudoyer.

Laure Hayman, now in her seventies, was very put out by the portrait of Odette de Crécy, who shared her habit of employing English phraseology; who, like her, lived in the rue La Pérouse. Proust, however, immediately came to his own defence and, it seems, in all sincerity:

'Not only is Odette de Crécy not you; she is the very opposite of you. I should have thought that every word she speaks makes this crystal clear. I have placed, in Odette's salon, all those particular flowers that a certain "lady of the aristocracy" as you call her, has in hers. She recognised these flowers and wrote to thank me without thinking for a moment that that made her Odette. You tell me that the "cage" (!) you live in resembles Odette's. You very much surprise me. Your own taste is so very sure, so bold! If I wanted to identify a piece of furniture or a material, I would turn to you immediately before any other artist.' The first volume had just been published when war broke out. This was a further obstacle in his path. A few dozen readers had had time to discover, with wonder and delight, what happened in the world *Du côté de chez Swann*. For the whole world, literature was now only a beautiful memory, a peacetime occupation. He was, however, to profit from the troubled times. It was true that, before the war, Proust's unchanging attitude was that of the Frenchmen of Saint-André-des-Champs.

Marcel Proust to Paul Morand: 'I am not going to talk to you about the war. It has become so much a part of me that I can no longer be objective about it. I can no more talk of the hopes and fears that war has brought me than one can talk of feelings that lie so deep they are a part of oneself. For me the war is not so much an object in the philosophical sense, as a substance that lies between me and objects. I live in the war, as men once lived in God ....' Marcel Proust, the man, never spoke of the war or the front except in terms of the utmost reverence, partly because he had always accepted the ceremonial and the conventions of his time, and partly because he was 'particularly sensitive to the idea of honour, and even the idea of the point of honour.' But while, as a citizen and a man of the world he behaved with deliberate conformity, as a novelist he was observing, without indulgence or self-deception, the collective passions which were so like those of individuals, and was noting the way human beings, and classes, and nations became distorted in these heady times. Proust pointed out to Lucien Daudet the hypocritical 'squinters' of the people at home, the special 'battle' tunics that the women wore and their high gaiters 'in imitation of those of our dear fighters'. He was exasperated by the stupidity of journalists who used words like 'Boches' and 'Kultur', who refused to listen to *Tristan* or the *Ring* and wanted no one to learn German. The war was being brought home to him on all sides. His brother, Robert, a medical officer at Verdun, was wounded early on and mentioned in despatches. Reynaldo was fighting at the front with a reckless courage *à la mort du loup* that dismayed his friend. Bertrand de Fénelon (the Nolenef of the Ocsebib), 'kindest, bravest and most intelligent of men' had been killed on the 17th December 1914. Gaston de Caillavet died on the 13th January 1915. Although he had long since been declared unfit for medical service because of chronic illness, Marcel had to undergo re-examinations from time to time. There was no question about his condition, but 'examinations are often hasty and imperfect. Reynaldo was an observer of one such examination: "What is wrong with you?" "I have a bad heart"—"Nonsense, you're perfectly fit for service". And the sick man fell down dead. It could perfectly well happen to me, but in my case, it would certainly not be the thought of going that would kill me. My life in bed, and I've lived like that for twelve years now, is much too sad for me to regret its passing'. What really frightened him more than anything was the actual timing of the medical examination, which might well rob him of the few hours he could manage to sleep. By a curious mischance, he was told to report at Les Invalides at half-past three in the morning. It was a clerical error, but it seemed to Proust the happiest and most natural of arrangements.

Under the Taubes and the Zeppelins his life of a night-bird went on as before. In the evening, to the accompaniment of the sirens, he would take friends to Ciro's, friends like, for instance, Jacques Truelle, a young diplomat who thought highly of *Swann*, and they had a wonderful conversation, with Proust talking of characters from history and from his novels, all in one breath: 'He would link the Maréchal de Villars with Colonel Chabert or Général Mangin, Doctor Cottard with the *Médecin de campagne,* Madame de Guermantes with Madame de Maufrigneuse. You realised that he was tired of seeing so many people and you suggested leaving. He replied: "Yes, I'm worn out, but isn't it infuriating we haven't said anything about the Cardinal Fleury and the d'Espards. You'll have to come back soon, and we'll talk about them, or Albertine, as you're so interested. . . ." He would be taken to his door, and even on the doorstep he would still be talking about his characters in the detached manner of Balzac. "Certainly not," he would say, "you mustn't think the Duchesse de Guermantes is a kind woman. She might be capable now and then of some minor kindness but even then. . . ." ' And on another occasion, later (to Guiche): 'The Duchesse de Guermantes is a little bit like the tough old hen I once mistook for a bird of paradise . . . when I turned her into a formidable vulture, at least I spared her from being taken for an ancient magpie.' 'Why are you so hard on Monsieur Charlus? When you know him better, I think you'll find him quite pleasant to talk to. I must admit his *charlisme* takes indecent proportions. But, the rest of the time, he's quite nice and sometimes quite eloquent. . . .'

On another occasion, he called for Marie Sheikevitch. 'This

evening,' he said, 'I'm going to carry you off! If you like, we'll go to Ciro's . . . but please, you mustn't catch cold. And whatever you do, don't look at my collar, if you see some cotton wool sticking out it's Céleste's fault. She insisted on stuffing it in and I couldn't stop her. No, you needn't call a taxi, I have one waiting outside. And don't worry about your feet getting cold, I have had a hot water bottle put in for you. How nice of you to wear this wonderful white fox . . . Are you sure you don't mind being seen with someone so badly dressed?' Then to the head waiter: 'Have you got some fillets of sole in white wine? And some *boeuf à la mode*? And some salad? And then a very creamy chocolate soufflé to follow?' (Marcel's guests almost always ate the dishes he would have had himself if his health had permitted.) 'No, no, don't worry about me, I eat very little. You could let me have a glass of water; I have some tablets I mustn't forget to take . . . And some coffee . . . good, strong coffee, I'd like plenty of that, if I may'.

Often, he would drive through the darkened, empty streets of wartime Paris to join the Princesse Soutzo at the Ritz and, when Paul Morand (her future husband) was in Paris, he dined with them.

Proust made notes at that time, for his novel, of the Paris night sky during a raid, just as he had once transferred to paper 'the stormy days at Balbec'. He described the aeroplanes, which he always called *aréoplanes* climbing like rockets to meet the stars, and the searchlights that moved slowly in the criss-crossed sky, like a pale dust of stars, or wandering Milky Ways, or shining jets of water, which seemed, in the clouds, like reflections of the fountains in the Place de la Concorde or the Tuileries. When Marcel was not well enough to go out, Henri Bardac and a few others might come and dine at his bedside off roast chicken and apple jelly. On one of his rare leaves Reynaldo appeared once at midnight as he used to do, and sat down to play Schubert and Mozart and fragments of *die Meistersingers*. Towards four o'clock in the morning, Proust asked for 'the little phrase.' Later Bardac asked Reynaldo where it came from. 'Marcel has added a little flavour of Franck, a little Fauré and even a little Wagner to it but, basically, it's a passage from the Sonata in D minor by Saint-Saëns,' said Reynaldo.

His Victory

On the 11th November 1918, Marcel wrote to Madame Straus: 'We have thought too much about the war together for us not to exchange a tender word on victory night, rejoicing that victory has come and feeling sad because of those we loved and will never see again. What a marvellous *allegro presto* in the ending after such a long drawn out debut and theme. What a dramatist Fate is, and that man should be its tool! . . .' He had been very interested in the crowds that day and they made him understand better the crowds of the Revolution. 'But, however happy this wonderful and unexpected victory is, we mourn so many dead that perhaps gaiety is not the form of celebration I should have chosen. I can't help thinking of Hugo's lines;

Le bonheur, douce amie, est une chose grave,
Et la joie est moins près du rire que des pleurs. . . .

(I am not sure if "douce amie" is right, it's in the last scene of *Hernani*).'

He was far too intelligent not to see the danger in this rejoicing. 'The kind of peace I prefer is the kind that leaves no bitterness in anyone's heart. But since it's not to be that kind of a peace and there already exists a desire for vengeance, then I should have thought it wiser to ensure that such vengeance was impossible to carry out. Perhaps it is being done. However, President Wilson strikes me as being too soft and as there is no question of conciliation, and never could have been, because of Germany, I would myself have preferred more vigorous terms; I am a bit afraid of a German Austria that will inflate Germany as the compensation for the loss of Alsace-Lorraine. But this is only speculation and I may not have properly grasped the situation. It is wonderful enough as it is! Général de Galliffet once said of Général Roget: "He talks well, but he talks too much." President Wilson does not talk very well, but he certainly talks far too much. . . .' His private life was still, as always, in a state of confusion. 'I have embarked upon affairs of the heart, without issue, and without joy, that give me perpetual fatigue and suffering and ridiculous expense. . . .' To cover his expenses, he would have liked to sell the dusty piles of carpets, the sideboards, chairs and chandeliers that were in his dining room: 'The quantity, I hope, will compensate for the quality, which is mediocre, and with the rising prices of certain materials, like leather and crystal, I may perhaps be able to do quite well with them. I have no idea whether bronze is fetching a decent price in the sales or not. If it is, I shall get rid of any pieces in my drawing room that I don't particularly like. And then I have an enormous quantity of silver which I never use, as I either have my meals at the Ritz or I simply have coffee in bed. . . .' Then there came a piece of very bad news (a masochist, of course, never lacks bad news; he manufactures it himself): his aunt had sold the house in the boulevard Haussmann in November 1918. Where was he to go in post-war Paris if he had no roof over his head? His health was very bad. In order to sleep, he was taking up to a gramme and a half of véronal every day and it left him, when he awoke, dazed and almost speechless, and although caffeine brought him back to normality, it was also destroying him. In this state, how was he to endure the noise of carpet-layers' hammers all over again? He had, however, handed over the second volume of his book, *A l'ombre des jeunes filles en fleurs*, to Gaston Gallimard who was intending to publish it at the same time as *Pastiches et Mélanges,* a collection of contributions to various reviews and newspapers. The second volume (later to be split into three) was so long that it seemed like a strange mass of closely packed material whose very strangeness was attractive but whose density was terrifying. There was no lack of favourable criticism. Léon Daudet launched a campaign to have Proust awarded the Prix Goncourt. Proust, while affecting a certain detachment, busied himself likewise and with considerable skill. He enlisted the aid of Louis de Robert, Reynaldo Hahn, Robert de Flers, and his campaign was successful. Finally, on the 10th November 1919, he won the prize by six votes to four against *Croix de Bois* by Roland Dorgelès. Gallimard, Tronche and Rivière rushed immediately to tell him of his triumph and found him

in bed. The judges had taken a long time to make up their minds. Dorgelès had fought in the war and he was deservedly popular in the literary world. Was it not perhaps unwise to give the honour to a difficult book by a wealthy amateur, rather than to him? There were many journalists who thought so, and the choice was not a popular one. But what did a few unfriendly voices matter? Proust had wanted readers and now he had them all over the world. He received eight hundred letters of congratulation. He wrote with naïve satisfaction to his old concierge at the boulevard Haussmann: 'So far I have only replied to Madame Paul Deschanel and to Madame Lucie Félix-Faure. . . .' In England, Arnold Bennett and John Galsworthy recognised in him the direct descendant of

Passionately fond of chamber music, if the longing to hear some came upon Proust it was not unusual for him to dash about Paris in an attempt (not always successful) to satisfy his desires. One evening in 1917, in the midst of the war he summoned the Capet quartet to play the Debussy work for his sole pleasure at his flat in the Boulevard Haussman.

Dickens and of George Eliot; no praise could have pleased him more. Middleton Murry, in an enthusiastic article, wrote that, for Proust, artistic creativity was the only way a personality could reach its full development; he talked of the ascetic, educative value of the book. In Germany Curtius wrote: 'A new era in the history of the great French novel opens up with Proust . . . he forces himself on our intelligence and demands our admiration as a giant among men. . . .' The Americans loved his poetic and penetrating humour; before long they would be treating Proust as one of the classics.

What was the explanation of the universal success of this difficult work? Was it possible that a vast and diverse public was really

And so the intricate origins of the musician Vinteuil are a composite with recognisable traits, in part of Gabriel Fauré, at the piano with the youthful Roger Ducasse with Louis Aubert, Mathot, Ravel, Caplet, Charles Koechlin, Emile Vuillermoz and Jean Hué looking on.

In the famous septet of Vinteuil there are illusions to Fauré's quartet.

interested in the people of Combray, in Madame Verdurin's salon, in the beach at Balbec? In spite of the evidence, French critics continued for a long time to remain unconvinced. 'How can we say that an author is representative of the times we live in when he has completely ignored our social struggles, when he describes a world that has gone, and who, between the worldly and the human, has chosen to describe the worldly? . . .' However, as time went by, the foreign reader saw more and more clearly that 'in France the giant Proust towers over the first half of the 20th century, as the giant Balzac towered over his own, the 19th.' What, then, was the significance of Proust's novel? Undoubtedly, his novel was, like so many others, the story of a generation. A chronicler of genius, Proust had trapped for ever the flavour of his time; he had caught its gestures, its attitudes, its fashions, and even the quirks of language. But his work went very much farther than that! The reader, curious about French society, can find it described in this great work as it was between the years 1880 to 1919, but intensified by a past that gave it its meaning and its beauty. Those who sought a comment on the rules that govern human behaviour could not fail to find it in the work of this, the most profound moralist to appear in France since the 17th century. And those who hoped, as the majority of the readers of novels do, to find a kindred spirit who had suffered as they had, found him in Proust and were grateful for the opportunity of coming close to those dedicated 'intercessors', which is what great artists are. No doubt the reality that he painted, and of which he had first-hand knowledge, was a very particular one but, if all men do not fight against the same evils, and if the solutions they find are not identical, they are all human beings and there are few who could be indifferent to this man who, in all sincerity 'follows anxiously the road to self-discovery, bumping into every obstacle on the way, stumbling into every rut and losing himself at every crossroad.' Like *Wilhelm Meister*, and more than the novels of Stendhal, *la Recherche du temps perdu* appeared as a work of apprenticeship, although, at the same time, like the *Essais* of Montaigne or the *Confessions* of Rousseau, it was a summing up of the human con-

'When the piano and violin call to each other like two cooing birds, I am reminded of César Franck's sonata.'

dition that embraced the metaphysical and the aesthetic. It is of such a high order that the English, the Americans and the Germans were not mistaken who rated this immensc autobiographical novel above Anatole France, Paul Bourget or Maurice Barrès, or any other French writers of the time.

In 1919 he had lost his apartment in the boulevard Haussmann, the last fragile link with his family and the past. His aunt 'without a word of warning' had sold the house, and the new owner, a banker, had decided to give the tenants notice. Any such upheaval was, for Marcel, a terrible drama. The house on the boulevard Haussmann was transformed. It was now the Varin-Bernier Bank and Marcel had to leave. 'Alas, I don't know what address to give you just now, for I am homeless. I am reduced to repeating the lines to myself "the foxes have holes and birds of the air have nests; but the Son of Man hath not where to lay his head". . . .' The actress, Réjane, heard of his tribulations by chance and offered him 'a miserable furnished flat' in a house she owned in the rue Laurent-

Vincent d'Indy, in the centre, also played a part in the portrait of Vinteuil.

Pichat, but he only stayed there for a few months. Finally, he moved into 'hideous lodgings' on the fifth floor, 44, rue Hamelin. This apartment 'as modest and uncomfortable as the rent is exorbitant' was very near the Bois de Boulogne, which brought on his hay fever, and was only, he thought, to be a temporary pied-à-terre. He was there until his death, leaving 'all his belongings', what was left of his carpets, his chandeliers, his furniture and even his books at the furniture store. 'You could not imagine anything more bare,

The grand staircase at the Paris Opéra.

more poverty-stricken,' says Edmond Jaloux, 'than this room whose only form of ornament were the notebooks that comprised the manuscript of his work and which were piled up on the mantle-piece.' Great festoons of paper hung from the walls. The hermit's cell of a mystic of the arts. 'When you are a little lonely,' he wrote to Robert Dreyfus, 'tell yourself that, far away, a Benedictine (I was going to say a Carmelite) of friendship is thinking of you and praying for you.'

Au Docteur Maurice Springer, avec
toute mon admiration et ma profonde
gratitude. Mary Garden.
Melisande -

In February 1911 Proust and some friends heard Mary Garden at the Opéra Comique in her rôle as Melisande in Debussy's masterpiece. The composer was, like d'Indy, another inspiration for Vinteuil.

And so, too, Wagner. This copy of a Renoir portrait, incidentally, was stolen from the Opéra in 1971. Jean Cocteau first met Proust at Montesquiou's in Versailles in the very early days of the young man's career. Boldoni sketched the gardens of Montesquious' Versailles home as well as having portrayed the great dandy himself.

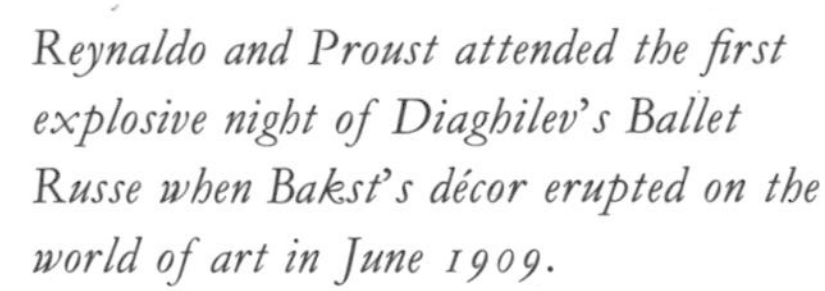

Reynaldo and Proust attended the first explosive night of Diaghilev's Ballet Russe when Bakst's décor erupted on the world of art in June 1909.

Helleu's sketch of hydrangeas for a wall paper design meant for Montesquiou. The comte was so addicted to those flowers that he was privately called Hortensiou.

The temple d'Amitié in what was Natalie Barney's garden in the rue Jacob. Proust admired this wealthy and talented American, who died in February 1972, but she was rather distant with him—a rather inexplicable reaction in one famous for her bizarre entertainments and proclivities.

The Last Room

Since 1913, Proust's household had been ruled by Céleste Albaret. She was a good-looking young woman with a fine figure, who spoke well and ordered her affairs with a kind of calm authority. She had come into Proust's life when she married the chauffeur Odilon Albaret whose taxi Proust had retained entirely for his own on those occasions when he went out himself or when he wanted a letter delivered by hand, or when in the middle of the night he had a sudden desire to see some of his friends and would send the taxi to bring them and take them home. Céleste had been instructed

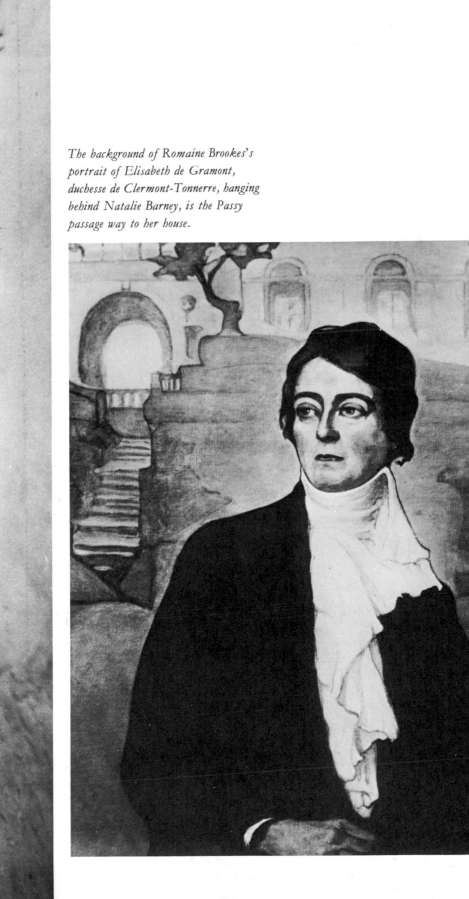

The background of Romaine Brookes's portrait of Elisabeth de Gramont, duchesse de Clermont-Tonnerre, hanging behind Natalie Barney, is the Passy passage way to her house.

ARRÊT · OBLIGATOIRE ·

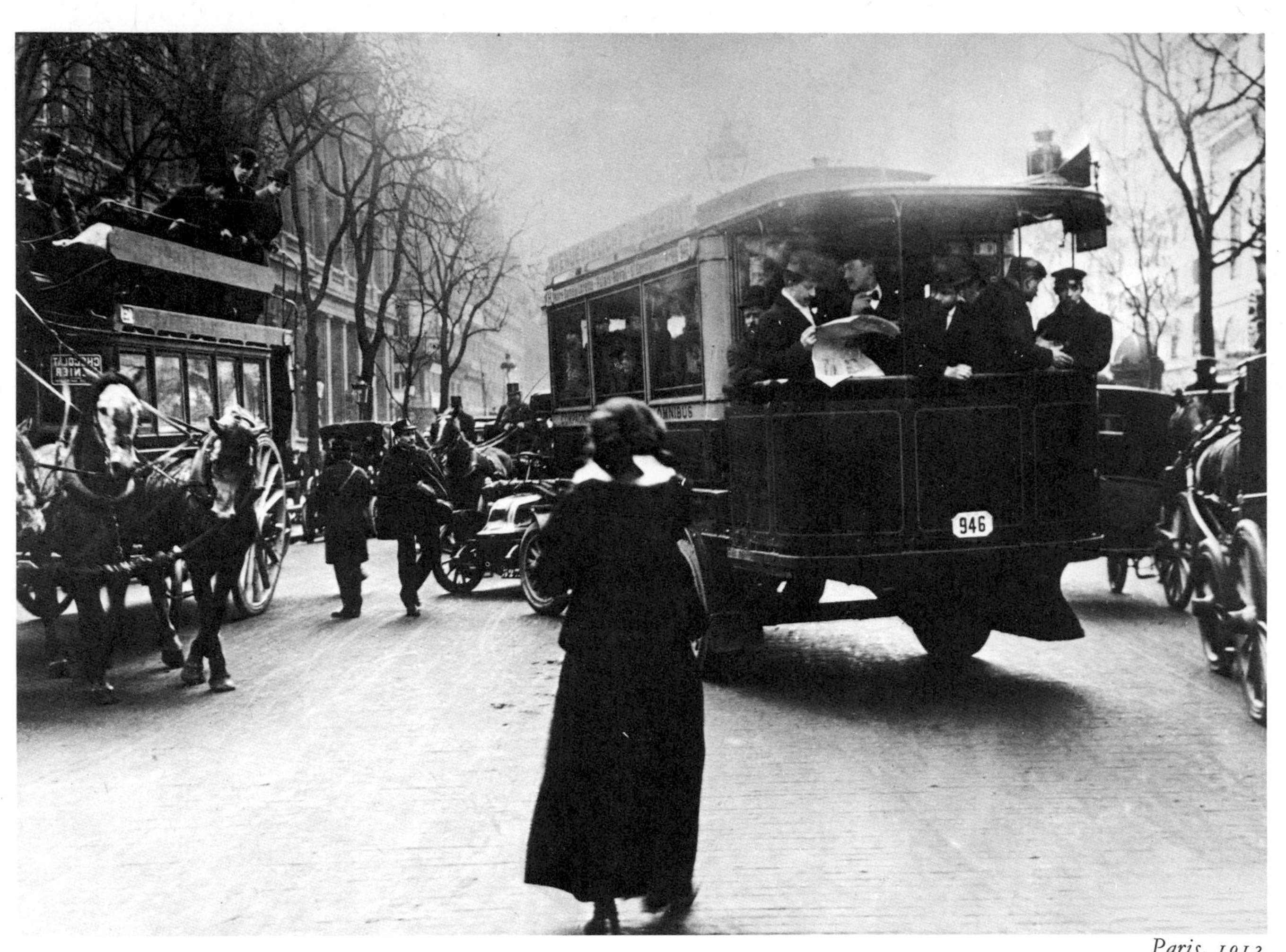

Paris, 1912

that she was never to come into his room unless he rang for her, which was usually around two or three o'clock in the afternoon. Then he liked to have his coffee waiting for him, as strong as Balzac had liked his; if he were slow to waken, Céleste might have to prepare two or three fresh brews one after the other, 'because,' he said, 'it lost its flavour.' Marcel lived almost exclusively on café au lait. Sometimes (very occasionally) he might fancy a fried sole or a roast chicken and he would send out to Larue's or Lucas-Carton's for it (or, towards the end of his life, to the Ritz Hotel). Cooking in the flat was forbidden as the slightest smell of it would precipitate an attack of asthma. The servants' meals were brought in from the Edward VII Restaurant in the rue d'Anjou, hence his enormous bills and the comparative poverty of this rich man. Proust would not have gas used anywhere near him, either for lighting or for heating because of its smell and he had had it cut

off. In all his letters he complained of a radiator that was too hot and brought on his breathlessness. Beside the bed he had a little bamboo table, his 'long boat' of old on which there was always a silver tray and, on it, a bottle of Evian water, a lime tisane and a candle which burned day and night so that he could light his fumigation powders. Matches were forbidden because of their sulphur smell. Céleste bought candles in five-kilo boxes. On the other side of his bed were the *Notebooks*, a few books to read, a bottle of ink and numerous fountain pens. 'He was,' said Céleste, 'a man who couldn't do anything for himself. If his fountain pen fell on the floor, he wouldn't bother to pick it up. If *all* his fountain pens were on the floor, he'd ring for me . . . His bed had to be remade completely each day and the sheets changed because he said the moisture of the body made them damp. When he washed, sometimes he used up to twenty or twenty-two towels because as

BAINS-DOUC
32
Bains Douches
OUVERT
Mercredi 9h à 19h
Jeudi 8h à 20h
Vendredi 7h à 20h
Samedi 7h à 20h
Dimanche 7h à 13h
Pédicure Manucure
Sudation
BAINS DOUCHES

In 1918 Proust more or less openly visited several male brothels, among them the hôtel Marigny and this Turkish bath in the rue St Lazare.

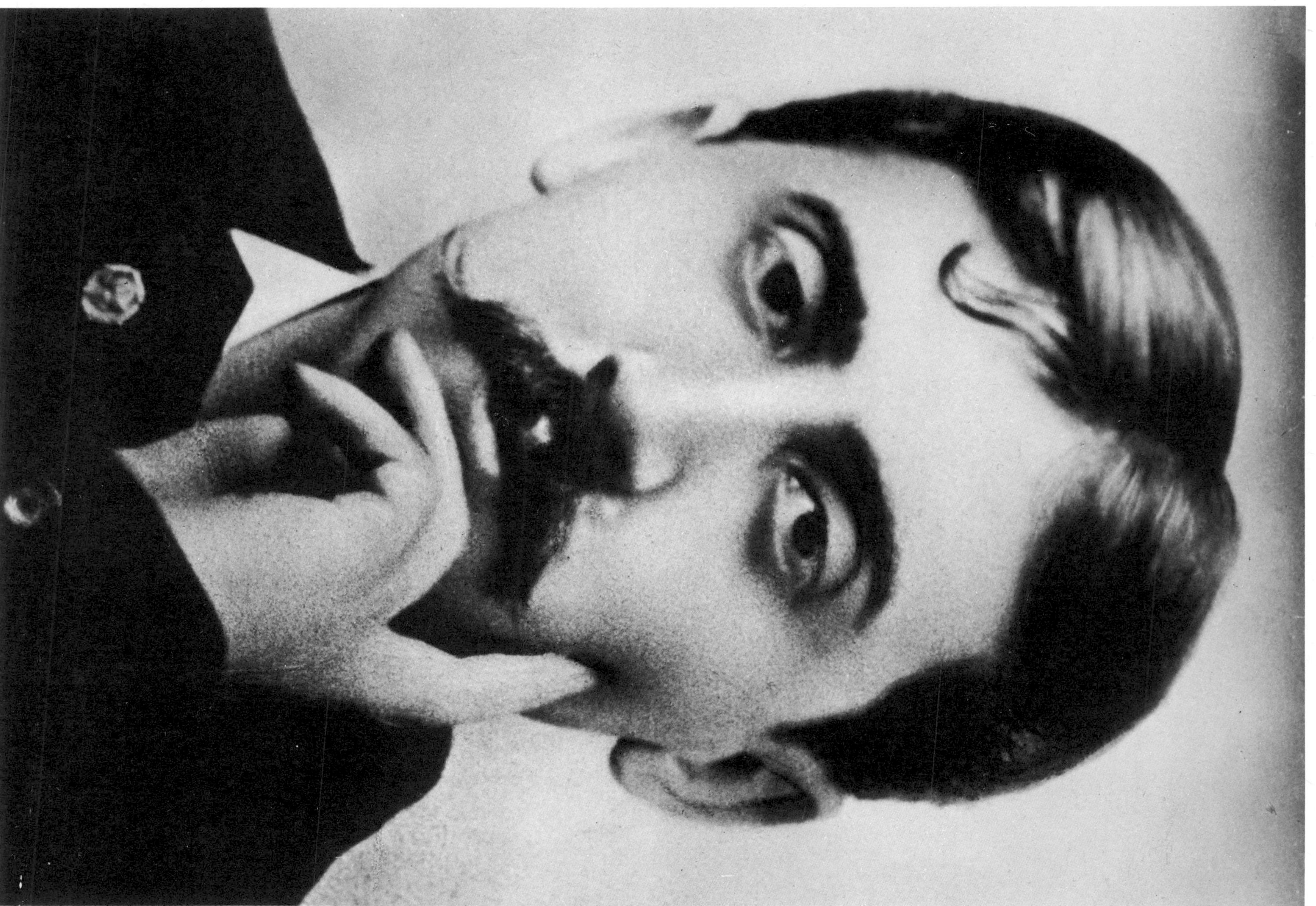

soon as one was wet or even damp, he wouldn't have it near him.' If Proust were working or sleeping, he was not allowed to be disturbed by anyone. Each day, he read his correspondence aloud to Céleste with a commentary from which she had to guess instinctively, if such and such a person were welcome at the house, if he wanted to arrange a meeting or if he were dining at home or in town. It was she who communicated with the outside world, making all his telephone calls from a nearby café, owned by 'people from the Puy-de-Dôme'. Céleste had adopted many of Marcel's ways, his phraseology and even his voice. She imitated his friends just as he did. 'The other evening, when she opened the door to me,' says Gide, 'after telling me that Proust regretted that he was unable to see me, Céleste added "Monsieur begs Monsieur Gide to be *quite sure he is always thinking of him*." (I jotted the phrase down on the spot). . . .'

After a while, Céleste had brought in her sister, Marie Gineste and her niece, Yvonne Albaret (who was a typist) to help her with

her work. Often at night, Proust would have these young women and the chauffeur Odilon round him in his room and would give them a lecture on French history. What would one not have given to have had a lesson on Saint-André-des-Champs, by the creator of that imaginary church and of the very figures over its porch!

Céleste never went to bed before seven in the morning, because Proust, who worked all through the night, insisted that she came the moment he rang his bell. At dawn, he would take his véronal, and then would sleep from seven in the morning until three in the afternoon. Sometimes, he would overstep the dose and sleep for two or three days at a time. When he awoke, it would take some time before, with the help of black coffee, he recovered his lucidity. By the evening, he would be brilliant as ever. Sometimes, Vaudoyer, Morand or Cocteau came to visit him. Having written a very favourable article on Proust, François Mauriac was invited to dine at the rue Hamelin. The day before, he received a telephone call: 'Monsieur Marcel Proust would like to know if Monsieur François

Simone de Caillavet, St Loup's daughter in the novel, later married André Maurois.
Her mother, born Jeanne Pouquet, served as a model for Gilberte, had married Gaston de Caillavet who figures largely in St Loup himself.

The make-up of Mme Verdurin's salon owes something to that of Mme Minard Dorian.

Mauriac would like to hear the Capet Quartet during the meal, or would he prefer to dine with the Comte and Comtesse de X . . . ?' Humble to the last even when he was famous, Proust could never believe that he could possibly be an incomparable attraction in his own right. Mauriac has described this dismal room, 'the empty grate, the bed with the overcoat serving as a bedcover, the waxen mask from behind which one felt the host was watching one eat; only his hair seemed alive. He himself was no longer partaking of the food of this world. . . .' Little by little, 'he was cutting the moorings'. He knew now that a writer's first duty is to live for his work; that 'friendship, because it is time-consuming, becomes a dereliction of that duty, an abdication of self; that conversation is a superficial distraction that gives us nothing.' Inspiration, profound thought and 'spiritual shock' are only possible in solitude. 'Love is even less dangerous than friendship because, being subjective, it does not turn us from ourselves'. Between 1920 and 1922, this very sick man produced a prodigious volume of work. He had ceased to

Forty years separate Marie Laurencin's 1927 sketch of Paul Morand, writer, diplomat and confidant of Proust, and the photograph of him and his wife the Princesse Hélène Soutzo.

Bertrand de Salignac-Fénelon 'whom no one who ever knew him could forget, the dearest of my friends, best, bravest and most intelligent of men' St Loup.

Charles Ephurussi's erudition and his article on Dürer were attributions bestowed on Swann.

be an amateur long ago, that is to say, a man for whom 'the search for beauty is not a profession', a dangerous state of mind, and he had become what a writer must become, a craftsman. His work was, in his eyes, a race with death: 'You will see, you will send me the proofs when I am no longer able to correct them. . . .' He would have liked Gallimard to have entrusted his books to four different printers so that at least he would be able to read them before he died. Had his health really deteriorated then so much? There were many who doubted it. His friends were used to his complaining and his suffering and had long since come to believe he was one of those valetudinarians who live to be a hundred. But Marcel was the son of a doctor and he was aware of disturbing changes in his condition. Like his mother when she was approaching death, he

Even as a very young man, when he first met Proust, Comte Louis Gautier-Vignal was known for his expertise in art and intimate knowledge of the great European and Russian collections. His step father, Sidney Schiff, under the pseudonym Stephen Hudson translated Time Regained.

Emmanuel Berl, historian and philosopher, corresponded with Proust during the war, but a fit of amorous inconsistency on his part ruptured the friendship.

often suffered from aphasia, he could not find what he wanted to say, he had fits of dizziness and would not get out of bed. One day in 1921, he wrote to Jean-Louis Vaudoyer: 'I haven't been to bed because I wanted to go and look at Vermeer and Ingres this morning. Would you be kind enough to accompany this corpse that I am and let me lean upon your arm?' During this visit to the Dutch Masters at the *Jeu de Paume*, he had an attack which he attributed to some ill-digested potatoes and which inspired the very lovely passage describing the death of Bergotte.

Thus, the umbilical cord between work and life remained uncut. A word, a look, a gesture, plucked at the wayside by the man who was coming to the end of his earthly pilgrimage with so much pain, dragging his feet and breathing with such difficulty, still

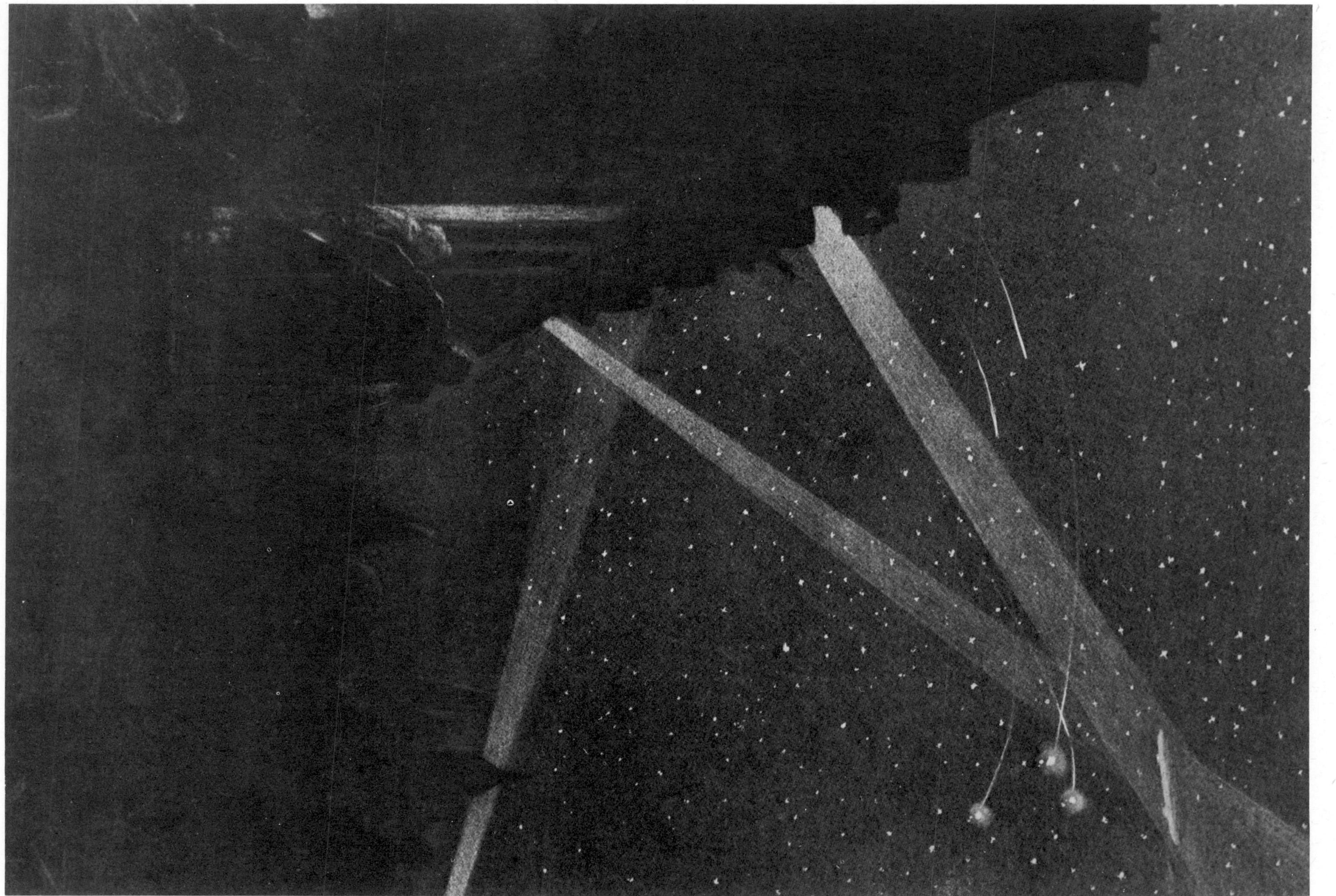

served to feed the monster.

Sometimes, he induced the impressions he needed. Once he asked the Capet Quartet to come and play to him alone, at the rue Hamelin, throughout the night. He wanted to listen to the Debussy Quartet which was to help him, indirectly, to complete the Septet of Vinteuil. He had hesitated about inviting friends and then had said to Céleste: 'No, I don't think so! If there are other people listening, I shall be obliged to be polite and I won't hear the music properly . . . I must have undiluted impressions for my book'. While the musicians played, he lay stretched out on a sofa, his eyes closed, seeking some mystical communion with the music as once he had done with Reynaldo's roses. He was going out less and less, but except when he was very ill, his seclusion was never total. He was still to be seen at the Ritz, dining in a darkened room, surrounded by servants whom he had taught to work the light switches, the positions of which he knew by heart. Boylesve, who met him at the meeting of the Jury of the Blumenthal Bursaries, thought he was seeing a ghost, a human version of the *Raven* of Edgar Allan Poe.

In July 1917 Proust watched a star encrusted sky swept with searchlights while the Germans attempted an air raid on Paris.

The mayoress of Soissons a cathedral town beloved of Proust, was renowned for her courage during the war.

Last Months

Towards the end of Spring 1922, Proust went to a party at the house of the Comtesse Marguerite de Mun, whose wit and natural kindliness he loved. There he met, for the last time, the friend of his childhood and his youth, Jeanne Pouquet (widow of Gaston de Caillavet, and now married again, this time to her cousin). After he had greeted a few people and scattered here and there protestations of devotion and of admiration ('He had an endless fund of compliments and little teasing remarks' said Barrès), he went and sat down beside her, and now that there was no further need to dissemble or to bend the knee, he let himself go in a great flow of comic judgements, acute observations and profundities, of the most elevated of philosophical reflections on the entire company present. 'He was very gay that evening and seemed in better health. However, when all the guests had gone, he begged Madame Pouquet to stay with him a little longer, and not to leave him so soon. But it was late and she refused for she was tired. His face took on an expression of indefinable sweetness, of irony and melancholy.

"—Very well, Madame, adieu."

"—Not adieu my darling Marcel, au revoir."

"—No, Madame, adieu! I shan't see you again . . .

"You think I look well? But I am dying, Madame, I am dying. Looking well?" and he laughed. "It's too funny! . . . (his laugh rang false and pained her), I shan't be going to any more parties. This evening has worn me out. Adieu, Madame." "But my darling Marcel, I can so easily come and see you one day soon or one evening maybe." "No, Madame, I'd rather you didn't come! Don't be hurt if I refuse your offer. You are kind. I am deeply touched but I don't want my friends to visit me any more. I have urgent work to finish. Oh yes, it's so very urgent. . . ." '

It was so urgent he felt he owed every remaining moment to his work. When Jacques Rivière asked him if he would write an article

RESTAURANT
15

The Ritz dining room during the war and Proust's private rooms. He wrote to Natalie Barney 'The Ritz is boiling hot—and I adore it. This place is the ugliest in the world (except for my apartment) but what's the difference?'

Gaston Calmette, the publisher to whom Swann's Way *was dedicated, was shot dead by the ex-mistress wife of the Minister of Finance, Joseph Cailloux, when he threatened to publish Cailloux's love letters.*

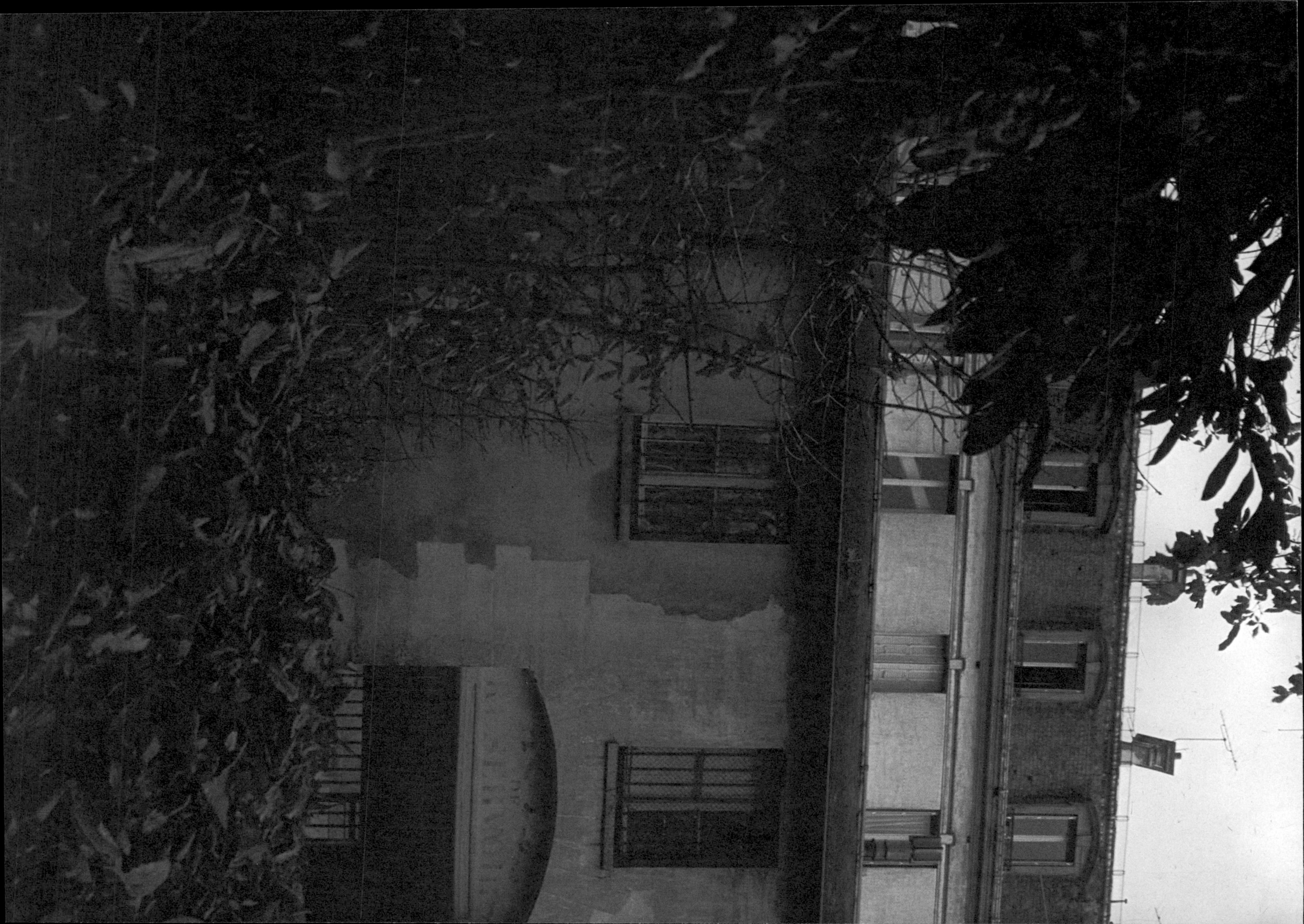

Grief stricken after his mother's death, in 1906, Proust isolated himself for several months in the Hôtel des Resevoirs in Versailles.

The actual château Guermantes. (overleaf) Prince Léon de Radziwill, himself partly St Loup, was the son Prince Constantin, the witty, somewhat forlorn perverse model for the Prince de Guermantes.

Jacques de Lacretelle when painted by Madrazo, was one of coterie of young writers, such as Morand and Cocteau who surrounded Proust in his last years, photographed last year in his flat.

Bernard Fay, author of In Search of a lost Soldier, *knew Proust during the war, and was a confidant of the sadistic practices on rats in which Proust sometimes indulged.*

Jeanne-Marie, Princesse de Broglie, one of Sotheby's Parisian experts is a descendant of Léon de Radziwill.

Armand de la Rochefoucauld the Duc de Doudeauville, is a nephew of Loche de Radziwill.

Paris, soon after the Armisitice when Proust was entertaining lavishly at the Ritz down the street.

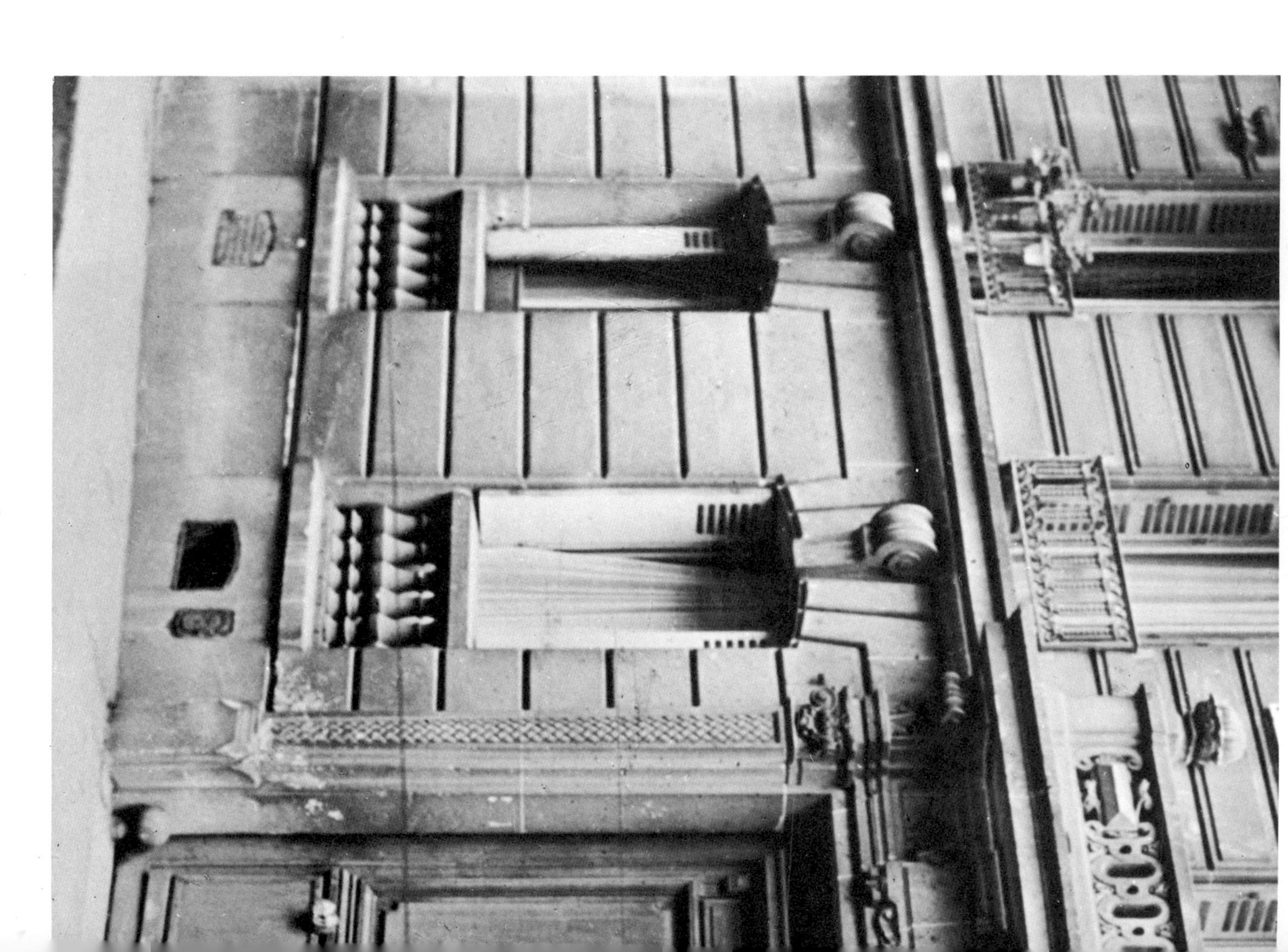

After he left 102, boulevard Haussmann, Proust took a flat in Réjane's house, 8bis avenue Laurent Pichat.

44, rue Hamelin, Proust's last home.

The study and drawing-room in the rue Hamelin.

on Dostoievsky for the *Nouvelle Revue Française* he refused: 'I have a passionate admiration for the great Russian, but I do not know him well. I would have to read him and re-read him and that would interrupt my work for months. I can only reply in the words of the prophet Nehemiah (I think) who was on his ladder when someone called him, I forget for what reason: *Non possum descendere, magnum opus facio.* . . .' 'I cannot come down, I have great work to do. . . .' He was in a constant agony of mind. For nearly twenty years, he had been struggling with images and words in order to express

Céleste Albaret, who appears in her own name, began working for Proust in 1912 and was with him to the end. Her husband Odilon was a taxi driver who kept his machine available, no matter what the hour, for Proust's use.

certain ideas which were to be his deliverance and at the same time be the liberation of all kindred souls. He was within sight of his goal but everything had to be said before he died. 'I had decided to consecrate all my strength to it, but my strength was ebbing away as if regretfully and as if to leave me just enough time, the circle complete, to close the door of the tomb . . . .' In June 1922, Lucien Daudet came to see him before leaving Paris, and found him looking even paler than usual; there were deep black shadows round his eyes. Lucien Daudet was embarrassed by the feeling that he was in the presence of a very great man and did not dare to say it to him. Marcel did his best to speak with the tenderness and humility of days gone by. Then they talked of one of his new friends and of the deep antipathy between him and the friends of long standing. 'Sympathies and antipathies cannot be communicated,' Proust said sadly, 'that is the great misfortune of friendship and of human relations.' A long time before he had written that friendship was more delusive than love. 'When I left him,' wrote Daudet, 'I felt the past rise like a lump in my throat. I wanted to embrace him; he drew back a little in his bed and said. "No, don't kiss me. I haven't shaved. . . ." Then I snatched up his left hand and pressed it to my lips. I can still see his eyes fixed on me as I stood there in the doorway. . . .' Throughout that summer, his health grew steadily worse. Someone had been stupid enough to tell him that the mind functions better on an empty stomach and so he refused to eat in order that *la Prisonnière* should be worthy of the preceding volumes. There was something sublime in this sacrifice of a mortal body to an immortal work, in this transfusion where the donor chose deliberately to shorten his days for the sake of the characters who were taking his life's blood. He wrote and told his friends that he was surely leaving them. 'And then it will be, really and truly, *le temps retrouvé*,' he added. In October 1922 having gone out at night and in fog to visit Etienne de Beaumont and his wife, he caught a chill which turned to bronchitis. At the outset, it did not seem too serious but he refused to allow himself to be looked after properly. He would not even allow his bedroom to be heated because the radiator impeded his breathing. Céleste, who was helpless and who was not allowed to call the doctor, soon recognised that he was much worse than usual, but he stoically continued night after night, editing *Albertine disparue*. Finally, about the 15th October, as his fever was interfering with his work, he consented to see his usual doctor, Doctor Bize. The latter announced that there was nothing very seriously wrong but that Proust should rest and, above all, should take some nourishment. Marcel remembered his mother, who had always cared for him better than any doctors and who was a firm believer in fasting. He maintained that food would only make his temperature rise even higher and would stop him going on with his work. 'Death is pursuing me, Céleste,' he said. 'I shan't have time to return my proofs and Gallimard is waiting for them.' 'He was very weak,' Céleste tells us, 'and continued to refuse to eat. The only thing he could bear was iced beer which Odilon had to go and fetch from the Ritz. He called for me every time he got breathless. "Céleste", he would say to me, "this time I'm going to die. If only I have time to finish my work! . . . Céleste, promise me if I haven't the strength to fight against them and they want to give me those injections that will only prolong the agony, promise me you'll stop them?" He made me swear to it. With me, he remained sweet and gentle but, with the doctors, he was so obstinate that Doctor Bize had to call in Monsieur Robert. The professor came and begged his brother to allow himself to be properly looked after, if necessary in a nursing home. Monsieur Marcel got very angry; he wasn't going to leave his room and he didn't want any other nurse but me. When the two doctors left, he rang for me: "Céleste, I don't want to see Doctor Bize again, nor my brother, nor my friends, nor anyone else. I forbid anyone to stop me working. You are to stay near my room, just you, keep awake, and don't forget what I said about injections!" When he said that, he gave me a look like thunder. And then he said if I disobeyed him, he would come back to torment me. But he told me to send a basket of flowers to Doctor Bize. That was always his way of saying he was sorry, if he'd had to hurt somebody's feelings. "Ah well, Céleste, that's one thing tidied up if I should die," he said when I told him the flowers had been sent.' This final

TURQUIE
DICTIONARY
L'U.R.S.S.
U.R.S.S.
UN AUTRE DE GAULLE

Mme Suzy Mante-Proust has for all the years since she knew her uncle adored him. Today she is devoted to his memory and his work. Always helpful to anyone with a keen interest in his books she is also most generous. One of the prize possessions of the Bibliothèque Nationale is her gift of her uncle's papers.

In 1972, fifty years after his death the Musée Jacquemart André held an extensive exhibition of memorabilia.

It was Jean Cocteau who introduced the young American photographer, Man Ray, to Proust's death bed.

André Brunet, president of the Friends of Marcel Proust and Combray.

Pour Madame [illegible] oyer [illegible] Marx.

Croquis que j'ai
fait d'après Marcel Proust
lit de mort.
En hommage et en souven

A. Dunoye

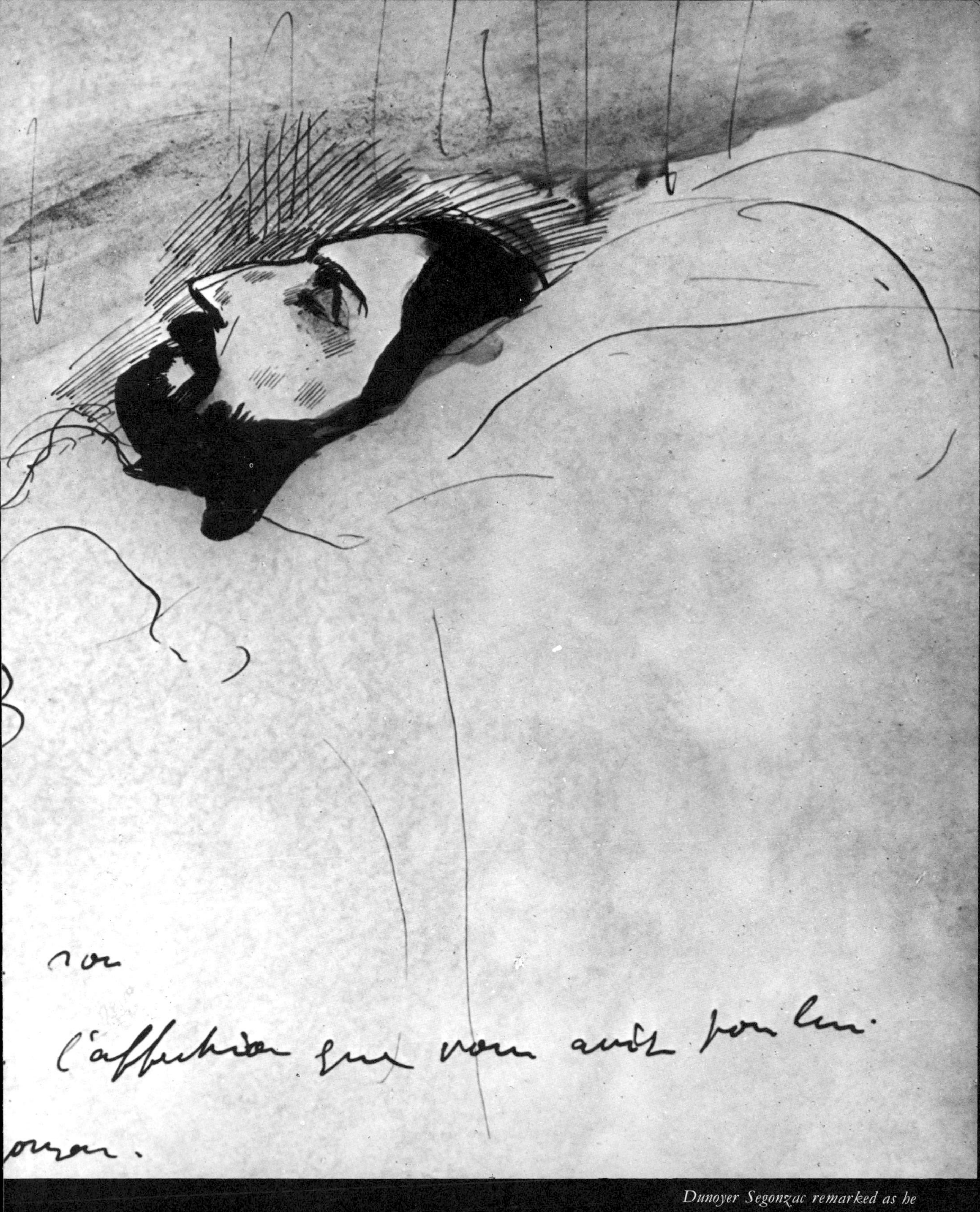

Dunoyer Segonzac remarked as he sketched the dying man that he resembled an El Greco.

Mme Cèleste, through the Straus family was until recent years the custodian of Ravel's home in Monfort-d'Aumury.

offering, floral and funereal to the god of medicine reminds us of the last words of the dying Socrates: 'Don't forget that we owe a cock to Aesculapius.' And just as Socrates, in his prison, sent for a lyre-player so that he might learn something even as he was dying, so Marcel Proust, knowing himself to be condemned by a judge as pitiless as those of Athens, surrounded himself as he lay on his death-bed, with books, his 'little bits of paper' and his proofs and added the final touches to the text that was to survive him.

On the 17th November, he believed he was getting better. He saw his brother for quite a long while and said to Céleste: 'It remains to be seen if I can survive the next five days.' He smiled and went on: 'If you want me to eat, like the doctors say, fry me a sole; I'm sure it won't do me any good, but I'll have it to please you.' Professor Proust felt it best to forbid the pleasure of the sole and Marcel knew his decision was probably wise. After another conversation with his brother, he told him he would spend the night working steadily and would keep Céleste in the room to help him.

His courage was unearthly. He made more corrections to his proofs and one or two additions to the text. About three o'clock in the morning, exhausted and breathless, he called Céleste over to him and dictated to her at length. 'Céleste,' he said, 'I think it's very good, what you've just taken down for me . . . I'll stop now. I can't go on any longer.' Later he murmured 'Tonight will show who knows best, the doctors or I.' About ten o'clock the next day Marcel asked for some beer to be fetched from the Ritz. Albaret went straight away and Marcel said it would be the same with the beer as with everything else, it would come too late. Breathing was now very difficult. Céleste could not take her eyes off the bloodless face, on which a beard had grown that accentuated the pallor of the features. He was desperately thin; there was an intensity in his

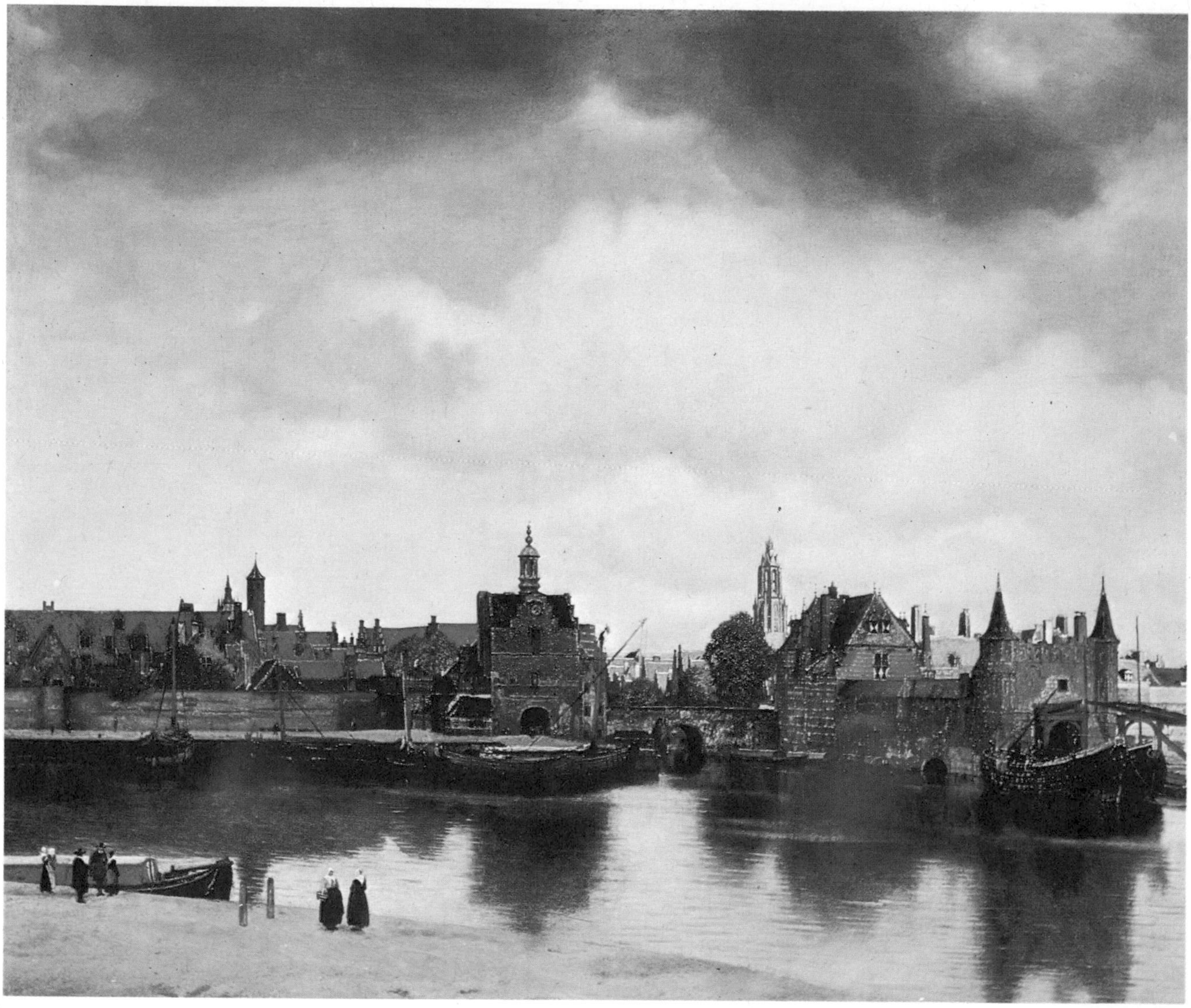

The last exhibition Proust visited was of Dutch Art at the Jeu de Paumes where he was photographed after seeing a painting he loved more than any in all the world, Vermeer's incomparable View of Delft.

The Château de Valière, near Morfontaine, the home of the Duc de Gramont.

ADMINISTRATION DES TÉLÉGRAPHES ET DES TÉLÉPHONES

TÉLÉGRAMME TELEGRAM P

CONTESSE DE NOAILLES
ACADEMIE ROYALE DE
BELGIQUE
BRUEXELLES BELGIQUE =

Déposé à = PARIS 46144 176 22º 10H12 = N

MADAME JE VIENS DE LIRE LE MESSAGE DIGNE DE VOTRE GENIE QUE AMBASSADEUR COMME LE FUT RUBENS MAIS PLUS PROFONDE QUE LUI VOUS AVEZ ADRESSE A LA BELGIQUE UN FAUTEUIL D ACADEMICIENNE A PARIS EUT ETE BIEN POUSSIEREUX ET BIEN OFFICIEL POUR VOUS A LA FEMME UNIQUE CETTE UNIQUE MISSION CONVENAIT TOUT CONCOURT A LA BEAUTE DE CE CHANT DU POETE QUI EMERVEILLE TOUT JUSQU A L ANNEAU NUPTIAL D UNE SOEUR QUI A OUBLIE OU PLUTOT RENIE MA FIDELE PREDILECTION LE NOM DE CHIMAY EST ENTRE MAINTENANT DANS LE DOMAINE POETIQUE COMME CELUI DE CHATEAUTHIERRY ET CELA GRACE A VOUS MON ADMIRATION QUI NE CHANGEA JAMAIS EST ENCORE ACCRUE PAR LES ACCENTS DE VOTRE CHANT SACRE JE BAISE AVEC RESPECT VOS MAINS QUI FURENT JADIS DES MAINS D AMIE ET JE DEMANDE A MADAME VOTRE MERE A MADAME VOTRE SOEUR A VOTRE MARI AVANT TOUS A VOTRE FRERE LA PERMISSION DE M ASSOCIER DE LOIN A LEUR EMOTION HEUREUSE = MARCEL PROUST 44 RUE HAMELIN PARIS =

The last walk he took from his flat in the rue Hamelin was partly passed in the courtyard of what was then the home of Comte Etienne de Beaumont, and now belongs to the Elie de Rothschilds.

Du Côté de Ferrières

Le Baron et la Baronne Guy de Rothschild
prient Madame Victoire de Montesquiou-Fezensac

à dîner le Jeudi 2 Décembre à 21 heures
On servira à 21 h. 30 précises.

Cravate blanche
Coiffures du soir

Les réponses sont attendues avant le 10 Novembre
10, rue de Courcelles
Tél : 41.68 & 49.74

Du Côté de Ferrières

Le Baron et la Baronne Guy de Rothschild
prient Monsieur
le Comte Robert de Billy

à dîner le Jeudi 2 Décembre à 21 heures
On servira à 21 h. 30 précises.

Cravate blanche
Coiffures du soir

Les réponses sont attendues avant le 10 Novembre
10, rue de Courcelles
Tél : 41.68 & 49.74

Du Côté de Ferrières

Le Baron et la Baronne Guy de Rothschild
prient Monsieur le Duc
et Madame la Duchesse de La Rochefoucauld

à dîner le Jeudi 2 Décembre à 21 heures
On servira à 21 h. 30 précises.

Cravate blanche
Coiffures du soir

Les réponses sont attendues avant le 10 Novembre
10, rue de Courcelles
Tél : 41.68 & 49.74

Du Côté de Ferrières

Le Baron et la Baronne Guy de Rothschild
prient Monsieur et Madame Richard Burton

à dîner le Jeudi 2 Décembre à 21 heures
On servira à 21 h. 30 précises.

Cravate blanche
Coiffures du soir

Les réponses sont attendues avant le 10 Novembre
10, rue de Courcelles
Tél : 41.68 & 49.74

Diner
du 2 Décembre 1971

Consommé Aurélie
Mousseline de sole Mahénu
Canard à la Madrilène
Salade Clarinda
Soufflé glacé Agénor
Friandises

Château Lafite-Rothschild 1965
Moet et Chandon Brut Impérial 1962
Château Yquem 1955

Marcel PROUST
1871 · 1922

(See preceding pages)

At one of the great costume balls echoing the court of Louis XIII given by the Prince de Sagon, memorialised in this water colour, Charles Haas can be recognised in the centre by his red hair and high ruffed collar. For many years it was thought the background was imaginary when in fact it is the Polish Embassy. The Proustian commemorative ball given by the Baron and Baronne Guy de Rothschild in December 1971 was an evocation of his own times and a testament to the fact that the World of Marcel Proust still exists as can be seen by the names of some of those invited, the seating arrangements with the evocation of places in the book given to various tables and the presence among many of Victoire Montesquiou-Fezenzac, grand niece of the great exquisite.

eyes as if he were trying to penetrate into the Invisible. Beside his bed, Céleste, who could hardly stand up (she had not been to bed for seven weeks), followed his every movement trying to guess and foretell his slightest wish. Suddenly Marcel flung his arm outside the bedclothes; he imagined he could see a hideous, fat woman in his room. 'Céleste! Céleste! She's very fat and very black! She's dressed all in black! I'm frightened of her.' Professor Proust was summoned from the hospital and came immediately. Doctor Bize arrived at the same time. Céleste, in despair at having to disobey Marcel's orders, watched as all the medicines, oxygen cylinders and hypodermic syringes were brought in. A gleam of irritation flickered in the sick man's eyes when Doctor Bize came into the room. Marcel, who had always shown such exquisite politeness did not greet him and, as if to underline his displeasure, turned to Albaret, who had just arrived with the beer. 'Thank you, my dear Odilon,' he said, 'for going to get the beer for me.' The doctor leaned over him to give him an injection. Céleste helped him to draw back the sheets; she heard him whisper 'Oh, Céleste, why?' and she felt

Marcel's hand press against her arm and pinch her in a final protest. 'Now everyone was crowding round him. They tried everything but it was too late. The cupping glasses could not longer hold. With infinite gentleness Professor Proust raised Marcel on his pillows. "Am I hurting you when I move you like that, my boy?" And, in a whisper, came Marcel's last words "Oh yes, you are, dear Robert." He died about four o'clock quite quietly, without a movement, his eyes wide open.'

That evening his friends telephoned one another and talked sadly, almost with incredulity, of the dreadful news. 'Marcel is dead.' Some of them came to see him on his death-bed. The wonderful, still, bloodless face, emaciated as an El Greco figure, lent an unbelievable dignity to this very ordinary, furnished room. 'His gaunt, sunken mask, darkened by a sick man's beard, seemed to be bathed in the greenish shadows that some Spanish artists paint round the faces of their dead.' A large bunch of Parma violets lay on his breast. 'We saw,' said Mauriac, 'on an envelope soiled with tisane the last few illegible words he had traced there, of which we could only decipher the name "Forcheville"; thus, right up to the end, his creatures had fed upon his substance and had drained him of what remained of life.' Suddenly, in this wretched room where a man blessed with so many gifts had just died, the meaning and the extent of the asceticism he had imposed upon himself, became clear. 'We suddenly felt,' said Jaloux, 'that he was far away from us, not only because he was dead but because he had lived a life so profoundly different from our own, because the world of searching, of imagination and of sensitivity in which he lived was not our world; because he had endured strange agonies and his spirit had needed for nourishment exceptional sorrows and meditations such as men rarely know. . . .'

'On his death-bed, he did not look fifty years old, and one would have given him barely thirty as if Time had not dared to touch the man who had tamed and conquered it. . . .' He had the look of an eternal adolescent. At the funeral, when he left the church of Saint-Pierre-de-Chaillot, Barrès, bowler-hatted and carrying his umbrella over his arm, met Mauriac. 'Ah well,' he said, 'so that's the end of our young man.' He was, above all and still is, our *great* man. A little later, Barrès acknowledged this. 'Ah, Proust, sweet friend, what a phenomenon you were! And what levity on my part to have passed judgement on you.' Having arrived at that moment when Marcel Proust's tormented earthly life came to an end and his life of glory began, it would be impossible not to quote his own last sentence in the description of the death of Bergotte. 'They buried him but throughout the night of mourning, in the lighted windows, his books, arranged three by three, watched like angels with outspread wings and seemed, for he who was no more, the symbol of his resurrection. . . .' At the Beginning there had been Illiers, a little town on the border between La Beauce and Perche where a few French folk huddled round an ancient church secure beneath its belltower; where, on fine Sunday afternoons, a nervous, sensitive child read *Françoise le Champi* or *The Mill on the Floss* beneath the chestnut trees in the garden; where he could see, through a hedge of pink hawthorn, the paths bordered with jasmine, pansies and verbena and stayed there motionless gazing, drinking it in, and trying to go with his thoughts beyond the image and the scent. 'Certainly, that corner of nature, that scrap of garden was not to know that this humble wayfarer, this dreaming child who contemplated it would one day immortalise its most fleeting moments.' Yet it is his exaltation that has brought to us the scent of hawthorn dead long ago and that has allowed so many men who have not and never will see France, to breathe in ecstasy, to the sound of rain, the scent of invisible but persistent lilacs. In the beginning was Illiers, a town of two thousand inhabitants, but in the end it was Combray, the spiritual home of millions of readers scattered today across all the continents, who tomorrow will stretch across the centuries—in Time.